How to Be Heard Without Screaming!

Find Your Voice and Use It Skillfully in 30 Days

Brenda J. Viola

To Dr. Judith D'Angelo, who taught me by example
how to be heard (without screaming)

Table of Contents

Introduction 1

DAY 1 - Silence Isn't Golden.................................... 3

DAY 2 - The Waiting Game (aka "Do a D'Angelo").....................13

DAY 3 - Clarity Is Key...19

DAY 4 - Buy Yourself Time 25

DAY 5 - Learning to Say No (Gracefully) 31

DAY 6 - The Power of Energy.................................35

DAY 7 - Read the Room (But Don't Take It Personally) 39

DAY 8 - Setting the Stage So People Can Hear You...................45

DAY 9 - The Difference Between Information and 49
Communication

DAY 10 - Serving up a Sound Bite................................55

DAY 11 - Choose Your Timing...................................61

DAY 12 - Nonverbal No-No's 65

DAY 13 - When Technology Doesn't Cooperate 73

DAY 14 - Dishing up a Great Message........................81

DAY 15 - Umm, Like, and Other Verbal Clutter...........89

DAY 16 - Anticipate Pushback 95

DAY 17 - Understand Your Audience.....................101

DAY 18 - Say It Again...and Again.............................107

DAY 19 - Bridge Over Troubled Waters 111

DAY 20 - When You Blow It...117

DAY 21 - Making Peace with Fear................................125

DAY 22 - The Method Matters.....................................133

DAY 23 - Make Your Messes Your Message 139

DAY 24 - And the Hero Is..145

DAY 25 - The Golden Rule...149

DAY 26 - Don't Say It!..153

DAY 27 - Ask For What You Want................................159

DAY 28 - Those Difficult Conversations 163

DAY 29 - The (Not So) Secret Ingredient...................169

DAY 30 - Lean In 177

BONUS DAY - "But What About When Someone's 183
Screaming at ME?"

Your Next Steps..189

*Want to Make Your Next Meeting or Conference.......191
Unforgettable?*

Want More from Brenda Viola?...................................193

About the Author...197

Acknowledgments...199

References..205

Introduction

Yes, there are volumes of books written about public speaking or communication tactics. And they're good!

But after years of people presenting me with sticky situations and asking me to help get them "unstuck," I realized there was a bridge that needed to be built between our professional speaking tactics and how we communicate in our personal lives.

In fact, I believe if you are a lousy communicator at work, you probably are at home, too.

Getting better at handling communication challenges will serve you in the boardroom *and* on Bumble.[1]

What follows is not a linear progression of do's and don'ts but rather a 30-day journey of ideas to consider. At the end of each chapter, you'll find a How to be Heard Exercise to strengthen your skills.

And like any good communicator, I've woven in stories to make this feel less like instruction and more like inspiration. In addition, these stories and lessons are in no particular order, so you can pick and choose topics that befit your current conundrum.

---

[1] For the blissfully unaware, Bumble is a dating app.

Reading this book won't solve your communication problems. But if you practice the principles contained in these pages, you'll get better.

And once you experience the thrill of successfully tackling a difficult conversation or finally holding a group's attention (and feel your message land), you'll want to do it again and again— and you'll keep getting better and better!

So if you want to find your voice and use it skillfully, then dive in, my friend. You're going to love the journey ahead!

— Brenda

DAY 1

Silence Isn't Golden

"…and when we speak we are afraid
our words will not be heard nor welcomed
but when we are silent
we are still afraid
So it is better to speak…"

— Audre Lorde

Chances are, you picked up this book because you are tired of shutting up and shutting down.

You might often fume about opportunities missed and replay conversations over and over in your head.

Perhaps you rake yourself over the coals for not speaking up. The long list of occasions where you chose silence comes with *another* list, filled with regrets.

I understand.

When the seeming comfort of silence seduces us and we succumb to its allure, the practice can become a habit.

The good news?

Habits can be broken if the desire to do so is stronger than the fear that fueled them.

When I see photos of me as a toddler and even up to age nine, I see an exuberant bundle of energy. If you dared visit our home, you were coerced to be in the audience, watching a show with me as the star performer.

It didn't matter that I weighed 100 pounds as a kindergartener.

I hadn't a drop of self-consciousness! Hand me a hairbrush for a "microphone," and I'd regale you with my lip-synced version of "Gypsys, Tramps and Thieves" (Cher's signature hair toss included).

On my ninth Christmas, my favorite present under the tree foreshadowed my eventual career. A tape recorder! If you came within earshot, I'd stick the microphone in your face and start interviewing you. When not interviewing my parents or sister, I captured my own voice, singing or pretending to anchor the evening news.

"Habits can be broken
if the desire to do so
is stronger than the
fear that fueled them."

I treasured those recordings.

But when tragedy struck the following year and I could no longer record my dad's voice, I simultaneously lost my own voice.

His sudden death, the product of one fatal, widow-maker heart attack at age 52, pulled the rug of security out from under our family. Salvatore Costello—the joyful, handsome, strong, and stable anchor to our home—left my mom and her two girls bereft.

My mom, who previously never had to make a living, was now alone with a 15- and 10-year-old to raise single-handedly. She placed an application at the local plastics factory—the only job for which she felt qualified. My sister and I intuitively knew to be very well-behaved and not add additional stress to a stressful situation. The apple cart had already been upended.

The result? A ripple effect of insecurities. The sudden and shocking loss of the anchor of our family (and the sole breadwinner) changed me from a lively participant in life to a silent spectator.

Instead of performing at family gatherings, I retreated to the shadows, nose stuck in a book. I became known as "the quiet one."

For my fellow quiet ones out there, I understand how easily you can be misunderstood!

"She's stuck up!" "What a snob." "She thinks she's too good for everyone else."

Quite the opposite. Even though there *was* a Cher impersonator inside of me longing to be free, my significant loss painted life as a series of potential failures. And I found it best not to try than suffer the pain of yet another loss. Or rejection.

When gripped by the terror of losing, you never engage in the game of life.

In high school, the trend worsened. My silence, perceived as arrogance, made me the target of bullies who would decorate my locker with chewed gum, stick insulting notes on my car, and bark as I walked down the hallway.

Yes, they literally barked.

It was a painful chorus that echoed in my soul for years to come. Oddly, it never occurred to me to fight back.

Their taunts only reinforced my desire to be invisible...and soundless.

Over a career spanning 35 years, I've interviewed or spoken with thousands of people from all walks of life. And do you know what I've discovered about those of us who have let silence define us at one point or another?

"When gripped by the terror of losing, you never engage in the game of life."

We either stay silent and invisible, or we choose to rebel.

When we choose to swallow our words for too long, they often erupt at inopportune times. The pendulum swings the opposite way, and, for fear of NOT being heard, we scream. If not literally screaming, we project our words as if they were written in all caps:

YOU *WILL* LISTEN TO ME!

In the summer between high school and college, I deliberately reinvented myself. Tired of being bullied and invisible, I embraced a bold, tough persona. This coincided with my new taste in music, when Devo and punk rock emerged as counter-culture to soft rock and disco.

My pompadour-like mullet, tinged with purple highlights and studded jewelry, completed the transformation.

Pat Benatar was my muse.

I carried myself in a manner that challenged, "Hit Me with Your Best Shot."

Oh, I still quivered inside, but appearances proved effective. No longer bullied, my persona created eggshells on which others should walk. Wearing the costume of confidence emboldened me to speak out against even perceived slights.

Attack, rather than be attacked.

No, it wasn't healthy. Because every bit, as much as my silent side, was fueled by fear.

Looking back over my shoulder, I see wince-worthy memories related to my aggressive speech.

Maybe you aren't a screamer, but is your communication style replete with complex defense mechanisms? Have you created an impenetrable fortress that results in one-way communication? Has it been said to you, "I can't get a word in edgewise!"

Or maybe you *do* scream. Like I used to.

Though never in professional settings, at home all bets were off. Anger felt better than powerlessness.

But it's not a healthy response to life.

After years of studying communication and making it my life's work, I realized my fatal flaw.

Like putting inferior gasoline into a luxury car, I'd been letting my fears, insecurities, doubts, and negative imaginations fuel my thoughts and sabotage my life.

What you continually think about ends up coming out of your mouth. And words? They are powerful tools that create your reality.

The good news? Just as my transformation into a pseudo-Pat Benatar was a deliberate decision, so too was my decision to deconstruct my false persona.

I decided to think, speak, and live from an authentic place.

The painful first step? Admitting to being a phony.

The next? Digging deep to discover my truth. And then to speak it.

"What you continually think about ends up coming out of your mouth."

As a professional communicator, it had been an easy cop-out to hide behind scripts. Scripts thrilled me! I could deliver them with authority.

Ah, but life isn't scripted, is it?

Don't you wish (like I sometimes did) that someone would arrive each morning with the perfect lines to say for every situation?

But you *can* be perfectly, authentically you.

You can be brave and choose to stop being invisible—first, to yourself.

Give yourself permission to have a voice.

And then practice using it.

HOW TO BE HEARD
EXERCISE

Look back to a moment in your history that served to silence or shut you down. Revisit the scenario in your mind and soothe the memory with compassion. Give yourself permission to speak up.

DAY 2

The Waiting Game
(aka "Do a D'Angelo")

"The wiser you become, the more
comfortable you are with silence."

— Maxime Lagace

Wait a minute! (I can hear you protesting.)

If you started this book at Day 1, you read my passionate plea to dislodge yourself from silence.

Then this chapter starts with a quote about being *comfortable* with silence!

Hang on; this story will help.

In 2004, our local chamber of commerce started "Leadership Main Line." As an incubator for emerging leaders, its sessions offered outstanding training in a variety of professional disciplines. From emotional intelligence to ethics, public speaking to philanthropy, the curriculum inspired. Only 20 individuals were accepted into each class, and I eagerly applied.

Once a member of this elite group, the jockeying began. Imagine a room of Type A personalities, all vying to be seen and heard, and to emerge as the alpha dog. As a professional communicator with a robust ego, I thought I had the competitive edge.

Instead, it felt like every time I opened my mouth, I became Linus van Pelt's schoolteacher, Miss Othmar. You might know her well from *Peanuts* cartoons (and if you don't, it's worth googling.) She is never seen and never heard, save for a *"wah wah wah wah wah wah wah"* trombone sound, inducing yawns and even snores from Peppermint Patty.

Banking vice presidents, marketing executives, restaurateurs, and attorneys all disappeared along with me into this same vacuum of blah.

Except Dr. Judith D'Angelo.

No matter the discussion, it seemed a marquee or bright yellow highlighter accompanied her words. She was the EF Hutton of our class.[2]

Rather than let her steal the spotlight for the foreseeable future, I invited her to dinner.

As the second glass of wine arrived, I blurted it out: "Judy, why do people listen to you?"

She smiled. And she had an answer!

---

[2] E.F. Hutton & Co., a Wall Street heavyweight 40 years ago, was best known for its advertising slogan: "When EF Hutton talks, people listen." The firm's ads featured crowds of people leaning in to hear the advice of a Hutton broker.

Many years have passed since our Leadership
Main Line class, but Dr. Judy D'Angelo remains
a beloved friend whose advice and example I hold
in high esteem. Plus, she sings a mean Neil Young
at karaoke night at the local Moose Hall.

"It's simple," she said. "When a topic is raised, I immediately scribble down my initial thoughts. Then I wait until everyone has spoken."

Shocking! My Arnold Horshack[3] tendencies ran counter to this communication strategy.

Judy continued.

"I then jot notes on what everyone has contributed and cross out duplicates from my original list. Usually, a thought or two

---

[3] In the 1970s show *Welcome Back, Kotter*, the character Arnold Horshack would wave his hand furiously and shout, "Ooh-ooh-ooooh, Mr. Kotter!" every time the teacher asked a question.

not expressed remains to be said. But before sharing my opinion, I summarize the comments of others, mentioning their contribution by name."

Scathingly brilliant, I thought! As Dale Carnegie said, "A person's name is to that person, the sweetest, most important sound in any language."

She concluded: "With each name mentioned, I've won the interest of my peers. Only then do I submit my idea for their consideration."

Drop the mic! Well played, Dr. D'Angelo.

Except, she wasn't playing. She never offered a synopsis that felt cloying or manipulative. Judy didn't flatter to win the day. She truly listened and respectfully waited to speak her piece.

I left dinner that evening knowing I had some work to do. This concept of self-restraint did not come naturally to me.

When you've endlessly heard "The squeaky wheel gets the oil," you become adept at squeaking.

But Judy D'Angelo proved that it's not always the loudest or most pervasive voice in the room that gets heard.

HOW TO BE HEARD
EXERCISE

In your next group meeting, restrain yourself from speaking, and jot down your initial observations. Listen intently to others, taking notes on key points raised. When everyone has said their piece, do a D'Angelo. And watch how people react.

"It's not always
the loudest or most
pervasive voice in
the room that
gets heard."

DAY 3

Clarity Is Key

"The great secret of getting what you want from life is to know what you want and believe you can have it."

— **Norman Vincent Peale**

After the dissolution of my 14-year marriage, I first wanted peace.

Then, I wanted someone's hand to hold while sharing sunset views and yes, taking those cliché walks on the beach.

Since the last time I really dated was in the early '90s, I wasn't just rusty. My flirtation devices were obsolete.

Plus, I was scared.

When friends dared to suggest online dating, I pooh-poohed this advice. Surely, I'd bump into someone at Whole Foods and sparks would eventually fly, leading to an exchange of phone numbers and my eventual happily ever after.

Many bags of groceries (and lonely Saturday nights) later, I finally surrendered.

My carefully worded profile description proved to be important for years to come. First, I had to really assess, "What *do* I want?"

Sometimes knowing what you *don't* want helps.

No unsavory characters, like Steve Martin's "wild and crazy guy" from '70s *Saturday Night Live* fame! I clearly stated I wasn't looking for a fling. Foreshadowing the theme of this very book, I stated the importance of being heard in a relationship. I wanted a good listener. And the ability to beat Wordgirl722 (my alias) at Scrabble would be icing on the cake.

As anyone who has dipped their toes in the online dating pool knows, some of those plenty of fish in the sea have stingers. The good news? It was easy to cull the good from the bad by how they either paid attention to or disregarded my profile manifesto.

The fish I eventually caught quoted my profile every time he splashed Brut on his freshly shaved face ("must smell good") or pointed to his crow's feet ("must have crinkly eyes from smiling so much"). The job description was clear, and he knew he was qualified to deliver.

And what, pray tell, does ANY of this have to do with this chapter?

I'm making a case for how **the ability to communicate well will enhance every area of your life**.

It's not just about serving up a rousing presentation at a critical work meeting or nailing the occasional public speaking opportunity. Improving how you communicate with a challenging customer service representative, your mother-in-law, a car

"The ability to communicate well will enhance every area of your life."

mechanic, or yes, even how you phrase your dating profile is basic training for the big conversations in life.

Clarity is the key.

If *you* are not clear on what you're trying to say or write before you open your mouth or start tapping on your laptop, *no one else* will ever get your point.

In addition, if you don't have a point or desired outcome, how will *you* know that you've hit your mark?

You won't.

So if you want to be a good communicator, figure out what you're really trying to convey first. Then work backward.

If this is a really important conversation, please be intentional and not loosey-goosey in your approach.

Once you have defined exactly what you want, determine what is and isn't negotiable.

No, this isn't a book about negotiation, but when you're buying a car, you know the absolute ceiling of what you're willing to pay. When considering a job offer, you weigh benefits and compensation and either accept or reject.

Why don't we stick to our guns with prospective romantic partners?

It could be those dreamy blue eyes, Adele playing on Spotify, or simply February. But stop that!

Life threw me a daunting curve[4] in 2021, and, after a healing period, I found myself back in the dating pool.

I knew the drill and was clear about what I wanted. Plus, I'm a writer with a successful track record of finding love online, so what could go wrong?

Some truly attractive counterfeits swiped right and ended up as lovely friendships.

Others seemed to fire on all cylinders, only to drop a bombshell. (For example, five ex-wives, extended unemployment, and in one case...homelessness. No joke. And no judgment, either. But that wasn't on my list of negotiable items).

Loneliness combined with nothing left on your Netflix watchlist can weaken your resolve.

And if you haven't decided in advance what is unacceptable, you'll put up with what should be a deal-breaker.

Let it play out without nipping it in the bud and believe me, you'll end up screaming for wasting precious time.

Whether in your personal or professional life, first be clear with *yourself* about what you really want. It will help the words you use, whether written or spoken, hit the landing.

---

[4] My beloved partner passed away. A story for another book. However, side note: Don't play around with your health. Go to the doctor!

HOW TO BE HEARD
E X E R C I S E

Think about a situation where you settled for less because you weren't clear with yourself (or with them) about what you wanted. Reimagine it with your new script.

Example: "Robert, you are a person with many wonderful qualities. However, I have clear ideas about my future, and living in your van is not one of them. I wish you well!"

DAY 4

Buy Yourself Time

"Life is 10% what happens to you and
90% how you respond to it."

— Charles R. Swindoll

One tricky thing about communication: it's rarely a monologue and most often an improvised dance with unpredictable others.

Sometimes these others step on your toes or deliberately push your buttons to get you to react.

Twenty-plus years after my high school bullying experience, I shockingly received a Facebook message from one of my former tormentors. It was replete with apology: she was now a mom and felt ashamed of her cruelty to me. Her humility struck a chord, and, of course, all was forgiven.

But I had to ask: "Why?"

To my surprise, she said, "Because it was so easy to get a rise out of you."

Aargh!

"When you're not
sure what to say,
commit to nothing."

Then I recalled tactics reporters would use to try and get "the story" when I was a public official. They'd ask questions completely off-topic or state a wild untruth just to rattle the cage of the person on the other end of the microphone.

Just getting the shocked or flustered look on camera or, in some cases, the angry "no comment" made for great footage. That out -of-context sound bite could make a story and break the target.

Most of us won't ever have *Action News* camping on our doorstep, but all of us will face a deer-in-the-headlights moment when we face requests, challenges, or unexpected situations.

It's not always a ploy to rattle or trip us up. But no matter the intention, it's unnerving.

What I wish I had learned in high school: Not everything requires a response. And most things don't require an immediate response.

When you're not sure what to say, commit to nothing.

One surefire, reasonable comeback is: "Interesting. Let me think about that and get back to you."

When a blatantly insulting question has been asked, maintain a blank look and respond, "Why do you ask?" (They usually fumble to respond, and you can peacefully walk away.)

As a former public information officer, much of my work was behind a microphone. In the early stages of my career, eager to please, I responded to every inquiry immediately. On the one hand, I respected the deadlines of the journalists trying to do their job. And on the other? I wanted to impress!

I soon learned that an unprepared response always got me into trouble.

I didn't realize that there was no shame in saying, "I don't have an answer for that." And I served my community (and my reputation) far better when I responded, "That's a great question. I'd like to do some research and get back to you."

Another benefit to buying time is that it defuses emotion that can get in the way of a measured response.

If it is burning on your tongue and you absolutely, positively have to say it? That's exactly the time to pause and give yourself a breather.

Apply this advice liberally! Not only in the boardroom but also at the dinner table.

We've all got buttons, and some people are excellent at pushing them. Not pushing back isn't a sign of weakness; it's strength.

In a famous passage from scripture, Jesus (who was a master communicator) found himself surrounded by an angry mob. Riled up because a woman had been caught in the act of adultery, they demanded a scathing condemnation from this so-called spiritual leader.

"Stone her!" they cried out with rocks clenched in their fists.

C'mon, Jesus! Show us that you're righteous by exacting harsh punishment.

It's easy to get caught up in outrage.

Yet, instead of speaking right away, the story goes that he knelt and spent some time writing in the sand.

Jesus was buying time and collecting his thoughts.

After a lengthy pause, he delivered a profoundly wise statement (a drop-the-mic moment, if technology had existed back then): "Let those without sin cast the first stone."

One by one, they all walked away.

Thoughtful responses will always win the day over knee-jerk reactions.

It's a matter of time. So don't be afraid to buy some!

HOW TO BE HEARD
EXERCISE

When asked a tricky question, give yourself permission to ponder. Even if it's not a life-altering or professionally important question ("Dinner Thursday night?"), practice saying, "Thanks for asking! Can I get back to you on that?" You'll discover how good it feels to buy yourself time.

"Thoughtful responses will always win the day over knee-jerk reactions."

DAY 5

Learning to Say No (Gracefully)

"Until you say no, your yesses will have no meaning."

— Denny Gilbert

"But what if it's my boss and I CAN'T say no?"

Denny Gilbert, quoted above, had a long and successful career as a dentist, but his true gift? At his core, he was a teacher. And he never tried to teach; he just oozed good advice and lived his life in a way that made people want to listen to him.

When he shared how saying no increases the value of your yesses, it was a true "Aha!" moment.

Because somehow, from the time I was a youth, I equated "no" with being difficult. As a card-carrying people-pleaser, I thought saying yes was the great elixir. Look how happy it made people!

Never mind how miserable it sometimes made *me*.

At a former job, I remember being put off by a particular sales rep who refused to work weekends. She wouldn't answer her phone or respond to work emails after hours. She outsourced whenever possible and brilliantly delegated tasks she found uninspiring.

The nerve!

I judged her work ethic. Compared to me, she was a slacker!

Yet she was one of the top performers in the company, winning an endless string of awards. The cherry on top? She actually had a LIFE.

Sometimes the very thing you judge is your best teacher.

We've all heard it said, "'No' is a complete sentence."

But since we're talking about the *art* of communication and the value of buying yourself time, it's not unreasonable to suggest massaging your no in a way that is more palatable.

Here are a few options:

- I can't say yes to this, but what I *can* do is _____.
- This isn't possible, but here are some suggestions to help accomplish this task…
- I'm going to have to decline, but can you circle back with me in _____ when the dust has settled?
- Is this timeline firm? Because I'd love to help, but my current bandwidth won't allow me to give it my best effort.
- I'm not able to take this on. Thank you for understanding.
- I appreciate you considering me, but I need time to think about this carefully.

"Until you exercise the muscle of 'no,' you will likely choke on the word."

Managing your time and energy is YOUR job as the CEO of you. No one can make you do anything without your permission.

Until you exercise the muscle of "no," you will likely choke on the word.

So why do we so often say "yes" when we'd much rather say "no"?

We care too much about what others think of us. I love the quote by Wayne Dyer: "What other people think of me is none of my business."

It's taken a lifetime for me to learn that there's a beautiful pay-off to spending time strengthening how I think and feel about *myself.* Finally settling my own worth emboldened me to only say yes to projects and opportunities that aligned with my core values and the life I wanted to live.

And buying time? Or saying no?

Quality people genuinely care about your well-being and happiness and will respect you for honoring your boundaries and bandwidth.

HOW TO BE HEARD
EXERCISE

Think about someone you regularly have difficulty saying no to. Is it a recurring request? Play the scenario out in your mind and prepare one of the graceful "no" responses in advance. Then use it!

DAY 6

The Power of Energy

"Nothing great was ever achieved without enthusiasm."

— Ralph Waldo Emerson

Students in Ms. Suzette DeGaetano's music class enjoyed a front-row seat to a one-woman dynamo performance in every class. You never knew what she would come up with, but it never failed to captivate.

She vibrated with enthusiasm.

Even before she opened her mouth, her platform heels, cascading (yet sky-high) hair, bright-colored clothing, and megawatt smile captured our attention. My sixth-grade class knew we were in the presence of star quality. Tina Turner–like in her demeanor, she taught way more than music. From *Soul Train* line dances to epic middle school plays, she championed creativity, cast shy underdogs to play starring roles, and offered fertile soil for our 13-year-old imaginations to flourish.

Best of all were the days when she would read aloud to us. True, this was long before teachers competed with electronic devices, but her keep-you-on-the-edge-of-your-seat recitation of the

"No one will ever
be more excited
about your content
than you."

epic *Scheherazade*[5] would blow any TikTok video out of the water.

Unlike Miss Othmar from *Peanuts* cartoons (referenced in our Day 2 chapter), Ms. DeGaetano electrified her audience.

You couldn't help but be swept up in her vortex of awesomeness!

Her joy in teaching was palpable as she savored every word and loved every student.

Such energy and enthusiasm are irresistible.

As speechmaker Carl W. Buehner so wisely said, "People will forget what you said, they will forget what you did, but they'll never forget how you made them feel." Forty-five years later, remembering Ms. DeGaetano[6] gives me goosebumps.

Truth be told, no one will ever be more excited about your content than you.

The game changer? Your attitude toward speaking. Do you see it as an obligation or an opportunity?

---

[5] The brilliant Sheherazade saved her own life by captivating the king with such cliff-hanger storytelling, he couldn't wait to hear the next chapter. After a thousand days, she finally ran out of stories. By then, the king had fallen in love with her and made her his queen. Talk about the power of communication!

[6] Suzette DeGaetano's other claim to fame? Mom to Suzette Charles, the first runner-up to 1983 Miss America Vanessa Williams. When Williams was forced to resign, Charles completed the remaining seven weeks of Williams' reign.

You may not be in a court of law, making a case before a jury. Your only audience may be the other camera square on a Zoom call! Still, that doesn't give you a pass to communicate on auto-pilot.

I can hear some of you thinking, "That's just not me."

I get it! (It wasn't always me, either.)

Yes, be your authentic self. But whether you have star quality or are happier out of the spotlight, you're *still* responsible for the energy you bring to every situation. Whether your style is quiet or effervescent, it can still be charismatic.

During a recent Zoom call with a client, the gentle, soft-spoken nature of his speech struck me. He wasn't selling anything, but I was buying. He oozed kindness and sincerity, and I hung on to every word.

The energy you emanate speaks louder than any of your words.

HOW TO BE HEARD
EXERCISE

Call to mind people who may not be on the cover of *People* magazine, but who, in everyday life, make you want to listen to them. What are some of the qualities they bring to conversations or other speaking opportunities? Are there commonalities? And mostly, how do they make you *feel*?

Next time you have an opportunity to communicate, don't just plan what you want to say. Consider how you want your audience to feel. Because that's what's unforgettable.

DAY 7

Read the Room
(But Don't Take It Personally)

"Don't take anything personally because by taking things personally you set yourself up to suffer for nothing."

— **Don Miguel Ruiz,** *The Four Agreements*

The opening keynote to kick off the 2023 school year meant a whole new audience I had always hoped to reach with The Public Servants' Survival Guide Workshop.

You can bet my cornerstone content was replete with facts and figures and an abundance of stories to connect with educators. Of course, I did a drive-by the day before to ensure I wouldn't get lost and arrived an hour before "show time" to ensure the room was ready for over 200 teachers.

But there are *always* landmines to navigate in live meetings (whether online or in person). Here are just a few from this one event.

The first three rows were completely empty, with the back wall filled with attendees who weren't "all-in" and preferred the company of their also skeptical colleagues.

Solution?

My go-to, a wireless microphone, gave me the freedom to walk through the entire auditorium, ensuring that everyone felt seen. By observing body language and facial expressions up close, I could assess where my message resonated and where it didn't, so I could adjust on the fly.

Next, Dan (not his real name) began interjecting zingers in full-on class clown mode. This can truly throw a speaker off their game because it interrupts the rhythm of their delivery. If ignored, it's like that mosquito buzzing around the room—a complete distraction (and boy, do you want to squash it).

Solution?

Dan became the star of the show. I literally stopped my presentation, walked over to him, and said to the crowd, "Why didn't anyone warn me about this guy?" They erupted in laughter (as did Dan), and I continued to weave him into every point that followed. Dan was comedy gold, and by me playing with him, the entire audience was won over.

But the real challenge?

The lone person in the FRONT ROW, yawning widely and loudly through the entire presentation.

This was not discreet, cover-your-mouth-with-your-hand yawning.

We're talking mouth-wide-open, audible sighing that signaled: "You are boring."

When you speak publicly, two audio tracks are playing. One track? The words coming out of your mouth. The other? The bubble over your head that no one can read (thankfully). It's a running transcription of your internal dialogue.

When your internal dialogue is too active, it absolutely detracts from your delivery.

So what was my solution?

First, I tried making direct eye contact, even directing a few of my points her way.

This evoked an even greater yawn. I swear I could see her tonsils.

Though tempted to devote the rest of my energy to engaging her, my wiser instincts shifted to the 200 other people in the room taking notes and nodding.

The phrase "Do not assume ill intent" clicked in. (Not making assumptions is also one of The Four Agreements outlined by Don Miguel Ruiz, quoted at the start of this chapter.)

Not taking things personally (the first of The Four Agreements) recognizes that *gulp*, not everything is about you.

Maybe this audience member had a screaming baby keeping her up all night. Or perhaps she's an insomniac who regularly stares at the ceiling at 3 a.m. Did someone switch out her high-octane coffee for decaf?

The potential culprits were many.

But none of them necessarily had anything to do with me.

Being super-prepared ensures that when things do go wrong (and they will), you are comfortable enough to improvise. Reading the room means, whether it's a packed auditorium or a small team meeting, you pick up on intel that could interfere with being heard.

As the speaker, it's your job to see and remove the obstacles.

And overlook the ones that amplify the voice of your internal critic.

HOW TO BE HEARD
E X E R C I S E

At your next meeting, pick up on the nonverbal cues of those in attendance. Where possible, make adjustments to make them more comfortable and engaged. And where impossible? Ignore!

"As the speaker,
it's your job to see and
remove the obstacles.
And overlook the ones
that amplify the voice of
your internal critic."

DAY 8

Setting the Stage So People Can Hear You

"A stage setting is not a background. It is an environment."

— Robert Edmond Jones

At the 2022 Fat Disorders Resource Society annual conference, it was my privilege to host a dinner to honor some remarkable women. Despite a chronic condition that involves pain, impacts their mobility, and is shrouded in judgment and shame, these women use their social media platforms to inspire and uplift others with lipedema.[7]

Though lipedema can impact the entire body, disproportionate hip and thigh fat is prevalent.

What does this have to do with setting the stage?

---

[7] Lipedema is a loose connective tissue disease impacting 1 in 10 women. It often presents at hormonal junctures, such as puberty, pregnancy, and peri-menopause. Despite diet and exercise, painful fat nodules grow, and if not managed, the condition worsens. You likely know someone with lipedema, though many remain undiagnosed. For more information, visit www.lipedema.org.

Caring about your audience, whether it's in an office setting, an auditorium, or a dinner meeting means knowing them and preparing in advance to ensure they are comfortable.

An hour before this important dinner meeting, I visited the private room that had been reserved for the occasion. The table was set beautifully. The décor, lighting, and menu were pitch-perfect. Soft music played.

But the chairs?

They had arms.

Most women with lipedema cannot fit into chairs with narrow arms. Can you imagine the awkward and embarrassing scene that would have ensued had we not been able to make the switch in advance of their arrival?

All of the compliments and expressions of gratitude might have been lost in the turmoil of correcting the environment.

Throughout this book, I'll make the case again and again that communication is in small part about the words you say. Everything you do (or don't do) communicates.

Anticipating your audience's needs and meeting them sets you up to be heard (without screaming).

Words that say, "I care" not backed up with actions that show you do are meaningless.

When you are the speaker (or the coordinator for a speaking event), you are also responsible for ensuring the environment is conducive to success.

At another conference, it was my privilege to coordinate a panel presentation. Because our four distinguished speakers would fly in from four different parts of the country, we had regular Zoom dress rehearsals to prepare. The content required minimal tweaking; the rehearsals were primarily intended for the speakers to become comfortable with each other in advance of the event.

Ninety minutes before the live panel discussion, I performed my normal tech check. Oh, the projector and microphones worked perfectly. But no laptop was on the lectern. The conference organizer decided that the A/V team would control the Power-Point from their booth in the back of the room.

Others on my team didn't see the problem, but as a speaker, I knew our panel would have two challenges not prepared for in our dress rehearsals. They would have to...

- Give constant verbal cues to the tech team to forward their slides.

- Continuously break eye contact with the audience to look at the screen behind them.

My initial, polite request was pooh-poohed. But I knew what was going to best serve our speakers and, ultimately, our audience.

And I didn't take "no" for an answer.

A laptop appeared! Our speaker team was able to perform as we had practiced. The delivery was seamless, impactful, and a great experience for both our presenters and our audience. And no one was ever aware of the behind-the-scenes struggle to make the environment conducive to success.

Whenever possible, set the stage in advance.

Once it's "go time"? Check the environment and adjust accordingly—and not just regarding technical matters.

If most people in the group are dozy and start shedding layers of clothing, there's nothing wrong (in fact it's very right) to ask, "Hey—would you like the temperature lowered in here?"

If you are an hour into a two-hour presentation and observe prevalent squirming, call a 10-minute break. Giving people a chance to stretch, get another coffee, hit the bathroom, or answer that text from their teenager will help them all focus when they return for part two.

Curating an environment that is conducive to listening will help you be heard.

HOW TO BE HEARD
E X E R C I S E

Notice what distracts you in a room when someone is speaking. Think of ways the environment could be improved, and make a mental note to adjust accordingly when it's your time to be heard.

DAY 9

The Difference Between Information and Communication

"The two words 'information' and 'communication' are often used interchangeably, but they signify quite different things. Information is giving out; communication is getting through."

— Sydney J. Harris

You wrote it! You said it!

But that doesn't mean your message was received.

Yes, your words may have even been important. But here's the fatal flaw: **Too often, we approach communication as an obligation rather than an opportunity.**

When you approach a speaking opportunity with dread, your audience will feel it.

It's not just the *audience* checking their watches or phones, waiting for the merciful end. *We* race through our own material as if rounding the bases, longing to be safely home (sometimes literally) and out of the spotlight.

Yes, you got through all your *bullet points*.

But you didn't get through to your *audience.*

What a missed opportunity!

Those who approach communication as a task to be completed (and survived) rarely make an impact. This is the critical difference between information and communication.

Every time you speak—or write—is an opportunity to be seen and heard (which may be what you find terrifying!). More importantly, it's your big chance to educate, inform, enlighten, uplift, clarify, encourage, remind, delight, and ultimately, serve.

How does one make the great shift from obligation to opportunity?

For me, it came when I started caring more about my *audience* than what they thought of *me.*

One of my most profound memories as a speaker involved a church service.

Five members of my bible college class were selected to speak on the topic of self-forgiveness. As I sat through speakers one through four, wonderful points were made and similar themes repeated.

I could feel the audience's attention waning.

It was getting late, and, honestly, most wanted to go home. Me included.

But it was my *obligation* to speak! I had pages of insights, just ready to wow the congregation!

"Too often, we approach communication as an obligation rather than an opportunity."

Mercifully, in the walk from my chair to the podium, I shrugged off my ego.

"You've heard so much about forgiveness tonight, there's nothing new for me to add."

I held up a piece of paper.

"Consider this piece of paper all of your failures, regrets, shames, and sins."

Then I crumpled it up, threw it behind me, and returned to my seat.

I'm not sure if it was the message of self-forgiveness that landed or the glee of relief that this long-winded service would be over, but I'll never forget the eruption of applause and the lesson learned that night.

Getting through my original notes would not have met the need.

Fulfilling my obligation as a good student? Wholly unmemorable.

But seeing an opportunity in the moment and seizing it? Caring more about my audience than "getting through" my outline?

Ah, the satisfying magic of true communication!

And once you experience it, you'll never settle for anything less.

HOW TO BE HEARD
EXERCISE

In the context of information versus communication, consider how to incorporate something unexpected that will surprise and delight your audience or team members (and stick the landing).

"Those who approach communication as a task to be completed (and survived) rarely make an impact."

DAY 10

Serving up a Sound Bite

"The more you say, the less people remember."

— **François Fénelon**

As TV news reporters, we used sound bites to tell complex stories in minimal time. Public figures were often blindsided by the two minutes featured on the evening news. "I spoke for a half hour, and *this* is what they came up with?"

The best interviewees pondered sound bites in advance. They synthesized their main message into a 10- to 15-second sentence that could be woven throughout the interview. That way, when the reporter was scanning for a prime cut, the main takeaway was clear.

We would do well to edit our messages in advance of any important conversation, presentation, or meeting.

What are you really trying to say?

When you first write it out, it could take up half a page.

Then start cutting out words.

Then cut some more.

When you've arrived at that one-line takeaway, you might think, *Ta-da!* But your work isn't done.

Just because you've got a clear takeaway doesn't mean your audience will hear it. Just like a golf ball, you've got to tee your sound bite up with what I call a verbal highlighter.

Don't you just love highlighters? (I do.) When you've been given a 10-page single-spaced report, it's easy to feel overwhelmed by the volume of information. But when each page has bright yellow markings saying, "Hey! This is important!" you take note. Sure, you might skim the rest of the text, but you zero in on the highlights.

It's the same with speaking. Here are some go-to verbal highlighters:

- The bottom line is _____.

- Here's what you really need to know: _____.

- It all boils down to this: _____.

- The main point is _____.

- The most important thing is _____.

In the *blah blah blah*-ness of many words, a verbal highlight causes the listener to lean in, prick up their ears, and take note.

Without a concise takeaway, important conversations meander and never get to the point. Meetings that could have been 10 minutes end up taking hours. A five-minute phone call could have eliminated an entire email string (and volumes of misunderstanding).

"Just because you've got a clear takeaway doesn't mean your audience will hear it."

One of my most impactful classes ever at Glassboro State College (now Rowan University) was also my toughest. Every Radio/TV/Film Communications major both dreaded and lived for Ed Kasuba's "Broadcast Journalism" class. Kasuba was the esteemed South Jersey Bureau Chief at KYW Newsradio 1060, the number-one-rated source of news in the Philadelphia market. Everyone listened two, three, or four times a day (a line taken directly from the station's ubiquitous mid-1980s commercial).

Everyone wanted to get an elusive "A" in his class.

Each week, he assigned us newspaper articles to rewrite for broadcast (a completely different style of writing from print media). The ground rules? Keep each story under 60 seconds. Use active rather than passive language and eliminate all unnecessary words.

One unnecessary word resulted in an automatic grade of zero.

The entire class, at least for the first few weeks, had a running GPA of zero.

But we got better.

The discipline Ed Kasuba taught served all of us in our respective careers. Though none of us became the next Diane Sawyer or Tom Brokaw, we grasped the art of being frugal with our words. We became accustomed to editing ourselves.

More isn't better.

During my years as a public information officer, ridiculously long meetings were the norm. On committee nights, department heads were required to "report out" key highlights. From public works to planning, libraries to parks and recreation, the multi-page agendas and comments from elected officials and the public meant "Honey, don't wait up for me. It's going to be another late one."

Sometimes we'd start gavel-to-gavel coverage of a board meeting at 6 p.m. and not leave the parking lot until 2 a.m. (No, I don't miss those days.)

Just as too many words get in the way, so too hefty agendas are an enemy of effective communication. So much is being said that most of it gets lost in the shuffle.

Keep your meetings on point and as brief as possible.

When giving a speech, always end on or before the allotted time.

Don't overexplain anything. It underestimates the intelligence of your audience and wastes everyone's time.

Here's a good litmus test: Are you trying to prove how smart you are? If so, you're probably talking or writing too much.

If you're trying to communicate, less is more.

HOW TO BE HEARD
EXERCISE

Practice incorporating a verbal highlight (or two) into your next important meeting or conversation. When you say, "The bottom line is..." followed by a definitive statement, watch how people lean in a bit and listen more carefully.

"If you're trying
to communicate,
less is more.

DAY 11

Choose Your Timing

"They say, timing is everything. But then they say, there is never a perfect time for anything."

— Anthony Liccione

You can have the perfect words. But delivered at the wrong time? It's like fingernails screeching on a blackboard.

We intuitively knew this as children. Mom in a bad mood? NOT the right time to ask for an advance on your allowance. Someone's team just lost the big game? Give them some recovery time before approaching them with a request.

My partner, Mark, taught me this concept when we moved in together. I worked from home; he didn't. Despite the companionship of Zoom meetings throughout the day, I couldn't wait to catch up with him when I heard his Harley rumble into the driveway.

I'd greet him and then go into a blow-by-blow account of...well, everything.

Mark was a master communicator, by the way. He lived by The Four Agreements, and when he was tempted to violate one of them, he'd disappear into his man cave (the garage) until he could respond kindly.

The garage-o-meter also let me know when I'd crossed a line or pushed a button. This wasn't a passive-aggressive attempt to make me see the error of my ways. He'd always (eventually) leave the garage and come back to me, calmly raising whatever issue had given him pause.

How refreshing! Because he was never trying to win or prove points, I learned that a healthy relationship could not only endure conflict but also become more wonderful after it. I felt safe with him and, in that safety, could hear anything he had to say.

And I'll never forget the day he taught me about "landing."

"Angel..." (Yes, he called me that. Even when I wasn't.)

"...when I come home, could you give me about fifteen minutes to just shake off the day and land a bit?"

Ah! Like a stretch-your-legs break between acts in a play. I could do that!

I learned a valuable lesson that day. When it comes to communicating with others—at home or at work—people need space. They need time to *land*. To get their bearings.

In fact, before starting most conversations, an excellent go-to phrase is "Is this a good time?" That gives people an out if they are on deadline, distracted, or simply hangry.

By asking, "Is this a good time?" you give people the opportunity to engage with you now or later. And that timing can give your message the best shot at landing.

Now, here's an important flipside to this message about timing: if you wait for the *perfect* moment, you could wait *forever*.

So ask yourself, "Am I waiting because the timing is bad? Or am I waiting because I'm afraid?"

Never let fear be the bully that holds you back from saying something important. If you've prepared, you have clarity about what you want, and the timing is okay—go for it.

HOW TO BE HEARD
EXERCISE

Start asking, "Is this a good time?" before heading into a conversation. It's a kindness that shows you understand the world doesn't revolve around you. And it can foster candor that can lead to better timing.

"Before starting most conversations, an excellent go-to phrase is 'Is this a good time?'"

DAY 12

Nonverbal No-No's

"What you do speaks so loudly that I cannot hear what you say."

— Ralph Waldo Emerson

During my career as a reporter, I remember interviewing a candidate for political office. Their perfectly coiffed hair, designer clothes, and list of talking points conveyed, "I'm ready for my close-up."

For all intents and purposes, they were.

Except for the eyes.

They avoided eye contact throughout the interview, and though I tried mightily to penetrate the fortress of this well-oiled product of a political machine, it was futile.

There was no spark of personality—not even a glimmer of humanity to be found.

I usually admire a good poker face, because I have zero game in this arena. It takes effort for my face to not show my hand. Invariably in meetings, team leaders pick up on my vibe and ask, "Brenda...did you want to add something?"

Aargh!

But give me an authentic grimace over a plastic mannequin any day!

Only 7% of communication is comprised of the words you speak. Then 38% is the tone of your voice, modulation, and pauses. A whopping 55%? Your body movements.

Body language is an important piece of the puzzle but far too often overlooked.

One particularly brilliant business leader failed to realize that every time he spoke publicly, his hand drifted upward and covered his mouth. He was the smartest person in the room, but this hand habit signaled, "I want to protect myself from my own words."

A gentle conversation and some practice broke that habit. But what nonverbal no-no's are *you* committing that might be saying more than the words in your script?

Let's do a quick body scan.

Eyes

- Don't avoid eye contact (because it looks like you're trying to hide something).

- Don't just look at one person or they will feel "picked" on (and the others will feel excluded).

- Do make people feel seen by scanning the room and letting your gaze rest on different individuals throughout the room.

- Do engage with those who are connecting with your message. These nodding, smiling audience members get what you're saying, and their body language is rooting you on! You can feed on that energy.

Hands

- Don't restrict your hands by holding them behind your back (or front, or side, or in pockets).

- Don't cling to a lectern or use robotic, overly practiced gestures.

- Use comfortable gestures as you would in normal conversation.

- Resist pointing, as it feels judge-y or threatening. If necessary, an alternate option is to use a gently cupped hand.

Legs

- Don't lock your legs or stand still (often a residual effect of clutching the lectern).

- Resist moving them excessively or pacing the stage unless you incorporate strategic body pauses.

- Allow them to be a natural extension of your hand movements.

- When making an important point, step forward to connect, then step back to give "space" for what you said to take root.

"The more you own
your message,
the more your body
will reinforce rather
than detract from
your meaning."

Posture

- Resist slouching your shoulders, drooping your head, or curving your neck. These convey insecurity.

Clothing

- Comfort is queen! Yes, look pulled together and appropriate for the situation, but when your jacket constricts you or your shoes pinch your toes with each step, these factors all work against good body language.

- Avoid black, white, stripes, or intricate patterns when on camera for television or video conferences.

Accessories

- Unless accessories support your message, like a pink ribbon worn during a breast cancer awareness speech, let nothing steal the show from your message. When my news director ordered me to ditch my big earrings because that's all she could focus on, I realized that fabulous fashion expressions were better suited to the Met Gala. (Of course, I'm still waiting for THAT invitation...)

- Before online meetings, clean up any background clutter. We all welcome it when a baby or puppy dog (or kitty cat) makes a surprise guest appearance. But let that be the exception to the rule.

The more you own your message, the more your body will reinforce rather than detract from your meaning.

May I also gently suggest that it is likely you aren't truly seeing yourself accurately?

When I went blonde several years ago, it never occurred to me that I needed to update my eyebrow pencil. Talk about a disconnect. So obvious! Yet so overlooked.

A savvy city clerk installed a mirror behind the boardroom door for commissioners to do a quick check before heading into a live, televised meeting.

The camera never blinks. Your audience is observant. And not everyone is kind enough to say, "You've got today's lunch still stuck in your teeth," or "Your zipper is down." How thankful I am for the kind souls who have alerted me to wardrobe malfunctions through the years.

If 93% of what you communicate is nonverbal, it would serve you well to have fresh eyes to coach you out of some bad habits. You might not even be aware of them, but they are usually easily corrected and can improve how people perceive you.

What you have to say is too important to be hijacked by a nonverbal no-no.

HOW TO BE HEARD
EXERCISE

Do an audit of your nonverbal communication, or have someone you respect coach you on ways to improve, from your clothing to your gestures. And don't hesitate to engage a pro. One of my favorite things to do is dislodge speakers from nonverbal bad habits and give them new confidence in person or on Zoom.

DAY 13

When Technology Doesn't Cooperate

"Technology is a useful servant but a dangerous master."

— Christian Lous Lange

In a classic episode of *The Office*, Michael Scott planned a dinner party to unveil his pride and joy: a new, flat-screen plasma TV.

The big reveal? A bust when his guests realized it was the smallest TV in the history of TVs. Definitely not suited for watching the big game (or anything, for that matter).

This episode came to mind when I arrived at the auditorium for a speaking engagement for 400 teachers.

My contract clearly outlined my technology needs, including a projector, screen, and speakers to play the sound from my video clips.

A wireless lavalier (clip-on) microphone is a must so I can use my hands to gesture freely and move through the room untethered by cords.

I also request that a tech pro be available to help work through any last-minute hiccups an hour prior to the live event.

You'd think I'd crossed all the t's and dotted the i's, right?

Upon entering the room, I saw a teeny-tiny TV in the middle of the huge stage. Completely incompatible with the hundreds of seats in the auditorium, it was clear that even those in the *front* row wouldn't be able to make out the images and words on my PowerPoint.

"It's the only monitor we had with sound," was the reply given.

With go time nearing, a quick decision was needed. I determined that the 80 slides with visuals were more important than the six video clips requiring sound. "Let's switch it out to the biggest screen you have."

Sure, I'd have to adjust around the missing video clips, but this was manageable.

The next speedbump? Clipping on the wireless lavalier microphone, turning it on, and "*SCREEEEEEEEECH!*"

Horrible, stomach-turning feedback. No matter what we did.

"Fine, I'll just use the handheld microphone."

You can't gesture with the hand that holds the mic unless you're willing for the sound to continually rise and lower in volume. So yet again, my game plan needed adjusting.

How I wish this were the only story in my history of speaking where technology failed me! From poorly timed internet outages to remote clickers that fail to move slides forward...I've experienced it all.

"Technology WILL fail you. But do you let it rattle you?"

But the show MUST go on.

Technology WILL fail you. But do you let it rattle you?

Knowing your material like the back of your hand pays off most when tech lets you down. The very worst thing I could have done was allow my audience to see me flustered and make apologies throughout my presentation.

Because honestly? They were none the wiser.

Your audience—whether it's in a boardroom with your boss, on a live webinar, or in an arena filled with conference attendees—*shouldn't* know your presentation in advance.[8]

The benefit? If your entire plan needs to pivot, they don't know they're listening to Plan B.

However, I *always* let a tech team access my work in advance. They'll pick up on common mistakes, like font compatibility. I learned the hard way that fonts used to build a presentation don't live on *all* computers. When fonts are missing, the laptop makes substitutions, which can skew your entire presentation. You can avoid this problem by using your own laptop, but what an awful feeling to see my hard work looking amateurish and poorly designed.

Make friends with your on-site IT professionals!

---

[8] I have a rule not to provide my material in advance. That way people can't get ahead of where I want to take them, they can't share my intellectual property, and if things go technologically south, no one knows what it SHOULD have looked like.

A beloved *QVC* show host was known to bring homemade baked goods to the tech crew when arriving for her shift. (She was a smart cookie!) They bent over backward to ensure she looked and sounded terrific each time she took the stage.

For those not speaking to massive audiences or on live TV, there are still the everyday tech fails that thwart your ability to be heard.

Let me vent a bit.

Pet peeve number one? People who continuously tap on microphones and bark, "Is this on?"

Ugh. Plus, it's a completely amateur (and annoying) move. You should have tested the microphone long before the audience showed up.

And online meetings? After all this time, why do people still position their backs against a window? When your face is in complete shadows, it's harder for people to follow you, even if they can hear you.

How can you *not* know that you sound like you're underwater? Do you test your audio? A good microphone is a sound investment in being heard. (Pun intended.)

Who can benefit from a ring light? Everyone! To my chagrin, many who *do* have a ring light place them off to the side. Good, *front*-face lighting highlights your eye contact and facial expressions—important components to your overall communication.

Stayed up late the night before? That little Zoom toggle "Touch up my appearance" can make you look well-rested.

"When technology turns on you, make it a part of the presentation."

Stay muted if you're not talking. And remember to unmute when you want to jump in.

Aren't we all tired of the chorus of Zoom faces saying, "You're MUTED!"?

If you're presenting a webinar, set it up to enable a practice session. That way you can work out any kinks before going live. And *use* that practice session with a fake audience to ensure they can see and hear you clearly. Don't forget to click that little box "Share sound" when sharing your screen, or the audience will see but not hear your video.

Whatever platform you are using, there are many online tutorials to help you become more tech-savvy.

When the world shut down due to COVID in 2020, my training work became 100% virtual. I became a Certified Virtual Speaker. In one hurdle to jump, the testing team replicated an internet outage mid-presentation. That's when I learned the importance of backup in the form of using my iPhone's personal hotspot.

And here's a tip that will serve you well: When technology turns on you, make it a part of the presentation.

I chuckle remembering that just as I made a crucial point, an audience member's phone suddenly blared Nelly's "Hot in Herre."

I waited. Paused and scanned the crowd with a smile.

Then said, "It sure is..."

A much-needed laugh ensued.

Don't over-apologize. Resist the urge to explain, "There should be a video right now..." Stay on point.

Serving your audience is job number one. And if it ends up being just you and them, with no bells and whistles, your content can still win the day.

Yes, technology *will* turn on you.

But it will never be more important than the message you've prepared to deliver.

HOW TO BE HEARD
EXERCISE

Do a tech check of your online presence. Is your face in shadows? Is your audio warbled? Can you test out "Touch up my appearance"? Just a few tweaks can eliminate barriers to being heard and help you put your best face forward.

DAY 14

Dishing up a Great Message

"At the end of the day, it's not what you say or what you do, but how you make people feel that matters the most."

— Tony Hsieh

Since good communication is an act of service, let's pretend we're sitting down to dine at a new restaurant.

You stand, waiting to be seated...and feel invisible. The host grunts a greeting and throws the menu at you. The specials are rattled off at breakneck speed (and in monotone.) Your water glass? Never refilled. Your entrée finally arrives, but the utensils don't.

The food might be great! But the experience? Completely uninspiring.

Then, there's Sonia Innamorato.

Sonia taught me the bliss of a meal served with unbridled joy.

When I was 12 years old, my 17-year-old sister began dating Sonia's brother, Tony. They lived in a Northeast Philadelphia rowhome—a complete departure from our rural, no-neighbors ranch home in Buena, New Jersey. Sonia's entire basement was devoted to meals. A long table could easily seat 15+ guests, and Easter dinner would last several hours.

First, the antipasto. There were heaping plates of meats and cheeses with exotic tastes like capicola and soppressata mixed with the sharpness of parmigiana, colorful olives, and crusty breads.

Then, bowls of rigatoni or fettuccine steaming with homemade red gravy[9] were delivered with freshly grated cheese and flecks of crushed red pepper. You got a pasta facial from the steam and wiped the bowl clean with more Italian bread. Even pre-pubescent me got a little glass of Chianti to wash it down and clear my palate for the whole turkey. Or roast pork. Or other kinds of meat or poultry that starred in the next course.

Had this been the era of cell phones, there would have been no texting at the table. This was a slow unfolding of gastronomic bliss.

You digested. Sonia would offer some fresh fruit to settle the stomach...before dessert.

Rich espresso served in little demitasse cups. A shot of anisette topping it off before dunking fresh biscotti in the inky goodness. Or creamy ricotta pie.

Sonia's glee in serving these amazing meals was infectious.

---

[9] Yes, gravy. It's a regional thing. My relatives all called the pasta topping gravy, drawing the ire of those who insist it should be called sauce. In remaining true to my roots, I had to use the word gravy here.

"Words should be delivered as if you are serving up a beautiful meal."

Now that you're salivating, know this: **Words should be delivered as if you are serving up a beautiful meal.**

Preparation first. Content must be gathered just as you would purchase ingredients for your feast.

Follow the recipe but improvise based on the specific needs of your audience or events of the day.

Set the table by making the room comfortable. Pick an appropriate environment for the conversation. If speaking to a crowd, don't shy away from amplification; embrace technology and media to add dimension. And if one-on-one, avoid mumbling or averting your eyes.

Offer seconds! In other words, don't expect everyone to grasp your point the first time you say a thing.

Don't rush your delivery. Let your words breathe like good red wine. Enjoy the power of a pause!

The more comfortable YOU are, the more comfortable THEY will be.

And the more you are enjoying yourself? So will your audience.

Just as a good meal should be savored, you can savor the content you're about to deliver.

When coaching a clinical professional, we reviewed her slides, which were filled with leading-edge medical information. This was a presentation packed with facts, perfectly appropriate for her audience. But as she practiced, it felt flat.

She covered the material beautifully. But something was missing. Sort of like pasta without the gravy.

Where was the elusive spark?

I stopped her mid-sentence and said, "Do you h
could use as a jumping-off point? What inspire
to this research?"

Her eyes lit up. She didn't need to ruminate. Her origin story was part of her DNA. As she shared the thread of curiosity that had led her to research and, eventually, remarkable improvements in patients' health, I knew we'd found the answer.

The passion she emanated when telling that story was contagious. She savored telling it.

And her audience ate it up.

Few things are as tasty to tell as a good story. And while facts engage the mind, stories help the audience connect emotionally with your message.

And not just with your message. With YOU.

Offering a glimpse behind the curtain, sharing a struggle and eventual triumph, or detailing a failure that led to a new discovery makes you a person, not just a presenter.

One of my favorite leaders always started our all-hands team meetings with a story about something he recently learned. Whether it involved coaching his son's Little League team or a podcast he'd listened to, these stories captured our attention and built a bridge that connected us. It was clear he enjoyed telling these stories, and because it wasn't forced or scripted, we all felt this authenticity.

I love research and stating facts and figures that can dazzle.

"While facts engage the mind, stories help the audience connect emotionally with your message."

But even better is when your audience *feels* something.

Remember, people will never forget how you made them feel.

Serve up a story and make your next presentation or conversation unforgettable.

HOW TO BE HEARD
EXERCISE

When was the last time you told a personal story when presenting to a group of any size? Give people a glimpse behind the curtain of your life so they can connect on an emotional level with you. And savor the telling of your story! The more you enjoy it, the more your audience will, too.

DAY 15

Umm, Like, and Other Verbal Clutter

"Silence is the sleep that nourishes wisdom."

— **Francis Bacon**

Nervous words are prevalent in everyday speech, and some are so commonplace they are hardly noticed anymore.

But they *do* detract from the potency of your message.

Can you imagine if this book read the way people talk?

Like, um, can you imagine if...like, if I were to write this book like, you know, like the way most people, um, talk?

Sigh.

Let's clean up that verbal clutter! You can...if you practice.[10]

---

[10] I'm not referring to vocal tics that are involuntary sounds or words. These can occur without a known cause, be part of an underlying health condition, or be a side effect of certain medications.

As a seasoned speaker, I thought I'd be the rock star of the local Toastmasters group.[11] I soon discovered that my speaking was peppered with throwaway words.

How did I know?

Because they COUNTED them.

Yep. Extra words were counted in each meeting and reported on at the end.

But why do we use these fillers in the first place?

Because we are terrified of silence.

Ah, silence! It's the very ingredient that gives your words room to breathe!

Don't you just love a comedian that milks a good pause...then BAM—the punchline?

The more you know and love your material, the more comfortable you will be incorporating pauses.

Pauses make sense when shifting from one topic to the next, or after you've said something weighty and don't want to rush on to the next idea.

Sometimes, I'll use the silence to "take in" the audience, scanning the crowd or table to take the temperature and read the room.

---

[11] By the way, because you picked up this book, you're likely serious about being a better communicator. Find a local Toastmasters group! Test a few out and see which one fits you best. You'll meet wonderful people and grow your skills in tangible ways. Plus, you can test-drive material with an unbiased audience who is rooting for you to improve.

"Silence recognizes
that communication
isn't a monologue."

Silence recognizes that communication isn't a monologue. When done well, it acknowledges the listener and allows you time to sense what should come next. Your script may say one thing. But taking the time to "feel the room" may offer intel that shifts your gears.

One of my favorite classes to teach is "Dealing with Difficult People." We ALL interact with challenging personalities, and my H-E-A-R-T method details what's going on *behind* the bad behavior to help achieve either peaceful resolve or agreement to disagree.

Halfway through my scripted presentation, I could feel tension in the room. I had a half-hour's worth of material yet to deliver, but a moment of silence and a scan of the audience nudged me to ask, "Before I go any further, do you have some real-life scenarios you'd like to talk through?"

Hands shot up around the auditorium.

The rest of our allotted time turned into invigorating problem-solving that the entire group benefitted from. (They'd seen similar difficult people in their respective offices!)

Instead of leaving them filled with angst about heading back to work on Monday, I was able to equip them with tools they could put to use in real life.

When you are hell-bent on delivering your prepared remarks, you can miss the opportunity for magic.

Magic happens in the moment—in real time when you connect with people.

The potential for magic is always there, but it lives in the space that silence provides.

Gulp down those ums, uhs, likes, and you knows.

The more you practice, the cleaner your communication will be.

HOW TO BE HEARD
EXERCISE

What's YOUR go-to verbal tic that clutters your speech? Make it a goal to be mindful of it and begin to edit yourself. Tell a trusted friend or colleague that you're working on cleaning this up, and have them help by holding you accountable in everyday conversation. Just like any other sloppy groove in our lives, you can break this habit, too.

"The potential for magic is always there, but it lives in the space that silence provides."

DAY 16

Anticipate Pushback

"There is no terror in the bang, only in the anticipation of it."

— Alfred Hitchcock

The meeting room at the local fire station was filled and overflowing with residents wearing grim faces. The murmuring increased in volume as the local government representatives entered the room.

To say I was nervous would be an understatement. As the public information officer, I'd be responsible for fielding questions not just from the audience of concerned citizens but also from the press. The first contentious public meeting of my career was about to begin, and I sure didn't want to screw up.

At the center of the controversy? Proposed construction to add square footage to the municipal building, originally built in 1926. A police building, added in the 1970s, proved woefully inadequate to serve the growing population and municipal services. Inefficiencies, like requiring residents to visit three different departments on three different floors to handle business, would be corrected with the addition. Our team, armed with pages of bullet points, took the floor, and you could feel the audience just waiting for their turn.

No number of talking points could erase the underlying—and valid—concern of these residents. The building addition would increase their tax bills.

And who wants *that*?

For us to pretend otherwise would be futile and even foolish.

Once the formal presentation ended, hands shot up all over the room. We listened to each comment and respectfully responded, but one citizen in particular decided an outburst was needed to ignite the audience. In a loud and rambling argument, he questioned the integrity of the project, ending with "This government needs to put a girdle on and just suck it up!"

I stood, nodding. In measured tones, I replied, "I understand your point, sir. But I have a question for you. Have you ever worn a girdle for an extended period of time? Because I have, and let me tell you, it's such a relief to take it off."

A bit of good humor mixed with the truth that we'd been sucking it up since the '70s helped to win the day. Completed in the early 2000s, the addition has served the community well for over 20 years and will do so for many more to come.

That winning line might have seemed off the cuff, and the exact wording was—but our team won the day because we anticipated pushback. We weren't naïve enough to expect cheers and applause, and hours were well spent coming up with every conceivable question and crafting respectful, fact-based responses.

You might say, "But I'll never need to speak in a public meeting!"

But you *will* ask for a raise.

Or attempt to work out a car-pool schedule with neighborhood parents.

And even balance your teenager's request for an allowance increase with the chores needed around the house.

Life is a series of negotiations. We make cases for refunds or forgiveness or time off all day, every day.

The smartest approach is to prepare for all the no's you'll receive well in advance.

One of my favorite programs of all time is *Parks and Recreation.*[12] Amy Poehler played the role of Leslie Knope, a perky, mid-level bureaucrat in the Parks Department of the fictional town of Pawnee, Indiana. My colleagues and I recalled bracing for season one, convinced it would make all government workers look incompetent. Surprisingly, though hilarious, they were full of heart—just like us! Knope, in particular, radiated with passion to serve her community.

A famous line I have quoted hundreds of times since she first said it on the show offers great insight into an angry audience: "What I hear when I'm being yelled at is people caring loudly at me."

People who don't care don't yell. Or ask questions.

---

[12] The series aired on NBC from April 9, 2009, to February 24, 2015, and if you've never seen it, catch the reruns on Peacock. Or google "How Leslie Knope handles a press conference" to see how she anticipated pushback and answered all the nasty questions her audience would have in advance of them asking!

Instead of being startled or offended by them, tune in to the fact that they care. Add in some empathy, and instead of putting them in their place, put yourself in their shoes.

We've already discussed at length the importance of having a plan, but make sure to factor pushback into that plan.

When I teach the workshop based on this book, participants pull out their real-life scenarios and, like reporters preparing for a press conference, come up with every possible argument to poke holes in their case.

All those questions help you anticipate the bang. And when the bang comes, your readiness means you won't have a deer-in-the -headlights moment.

HOW TO BE HEARD
EXERCISE

Prepare for your next important "ask" as if it were a press conference. Bring in an outside perspective or two to come up with questions you'd never consider.

"Instead of putting them in their place, put yourself in their shoes."

DAY 17

Understand Your Audience

"There is a great difference between knowing and understanding: you can know a lot about something and not really understand it."

— Charles Kettering

Mrs. Helen Dodge taught sixth-grade English, and she changed my life. Each Friday was creative writing day, and we'd read aloud the stories we created. While most of my classmates shrunk to be invisible, I always wanted her to call on me!

Though I was the last to be chosen for teams in gym class, a mediocre math student, and a complete failure at both home economics and woodshop, my star shone brightly in English class, especially on Fridays.

Why?

Because one day, Mrs. Dodge said in front of everyone, "Brenda, you are a great writer."

I latched on to that praise like a fly on sticky paper. Something I was good at! And I liked it, too? Like a lifeline thrown to a sinking swimmer, my spirits were buoyed, and it set the course for my future career.

"People want to be seen, heard, and acknowledged in a way that demonstrates you care enough to understand them."

I silently say, "Thank you, Mrs. Dodge," with each book that I sign.

She is the star of The Public Servants' Survival Guide Workshop when my audience is filled with teachers.

But when my audience is filled with municipal clerks, they never learned about Mrs. Dodge.

The star of *their* show is Eileen Trainer, the beloved former township clerk from Lower Merion, Pennsylvania. She taught me everything I know about public service while gracefully handling open records requests, recording minutes, organizing ribbon-cuttings, and charming cranky citizens.

Why? Because while some stories are relatable to any audience, every story lands better when it's tailored to the group that's assembled. Teacher stories for teachers. Municipal clerk stories for municipal clerks.

Let's take it one step further, though.

Knowing a person means having some basic details like a name, house, or profession.

Understanding a person goes deeper. It considers emotions, character, state of mind, and mindset. These factors offer important context that can make or break your message.

For example, in the midst of the COVID-19 pandemic, most in-person events were canceled. And many people were relegated to working or schooling from home. Zoom meetings were in, but they just didn't cut it for camaraderie.

So when I was asked to deliver the opening keynote for one of the first in-person international conferences since the pandemic, the organizers asked me to build on the joy and relief of gathering once again.

And I wanted to!

But heading straight to the celebration felt tone-deaf to me.

How many of our audience members had the agonizing experience of waving at elderly loved ones from a window because visitors weren't allowed in their assisted living facilities?

What devastating impacts were felt by small businesses and incomes that diminished, as did ways of life?

And worse, how many people were no longer filling these conference seats because they had lost their very lives? The collective pain needed to be recognized first.

After all, people want to be seen, heard, and acknowledged in a way that demonstrates you care enough to understand them.

So in my address, I went to the valley first...but I didn't stay there. Instead, once people knew I understood and respected the anxiety they felt, I was able to raise us all out of the valley on our way to the rousing mountaintop.

This concept of understanding your audience works even if it is a one-on-one. The goal is to build a bridge, establish common ground, and show you care enough to know some stuff! Take some time to dig around a bit. Whether they are an avid golf lover, dog aficionado, foodie, or newly engaged partner, adding in the personal touch will make your audience far more inclined to hear you.

HOW TO BE HEARD
EXERCISE

When preparing for your next important meeting or conversation, consider something "out-of-the-box" that shows you care enough to know your audience (without being stalker-like or creepy). Weave this personal touch into the conversation and watch how it breaks the ice and creates connection.

DAY 18

Say It Again...and Again

"The eight laws of learning are explanation, demonstration, imitation, repetition, repetition, repetition, repetition, and repetition."

— John Wooden

Empty seats. No-shows. Proclamations of "You never TOLD me!"

These are byproducts of a fatal communication error: fear of overcommunicating.

"But I don't want to nag..."

Believe me. They're not going to hear you the first, second, or probably third time you say it.

The Marketing Rule of 7 claims prospects need to hear a message at least seven times before they take action. In a blog written by American Express for its business customers, even more was recommended. "You'll get tired of your message long before your client does." (Just replace the word "client" with "audience," and this advice works for any situation.)

"If people in your life are yelling a lot, check your quality and quantity of communication."

This speaks to the heart of why we *don't* say it again...and again.

We think everyone else is bored.

Studies have proven that, after the first time we hear something, we forget 40% of what we learned within 20 minutes. After an hour? We've lost more than 70%!

Here's additional insight: "The less people know, the more they yell." (Rollo May)[13]

If people in your life are yelling a lot, check your quality and quantity of communication.

So how do you repeat yourself *without* nagging?

It's all in your tone and body language. If you utter the words through clenched teeth, use a red pen and all caps, or deliver the message as a reprimand for all the OTHER times they forgot, defense shields will go up.

Remember, the title of the book is *How to Be Heard **Without Screaming!***

Deliver your reminders devoid of emotion, judgment, or sarcasm. Just as your doctor's office sends multiple alerts for your upcoming appointment (without nagging), you're simply providing a service. Giving people the benefit of the doubt shows up in your tone. They can feel it and are more likely to retain and respond.

---

[13] Rollo May was an American existential psychologist and author of the influential book *Love and Will* (1969).

HOW TO BE HEARD
EXERCISE

When communicating something important in either your personal or professional life, practice using a few different methods to aid retention. Consider your audience! Don't just tell your spouse about those dinner plans on Saturday night. Send a calendar invite with automatic reminders or kick it old school and put a sticky note on their car dashboard, too.

DAY 19

Bridge Over Troubled Waters

"Ninety percent of success is not getting distracted."

— Shane Parrish

It was my first staff meeting as the leader of a non-profit organization, and my goal was to inspire the group, outline our objectives for the year, and set the tone for camaraderie and collaboration.

Unexpectedly, a cranky member of the board decided to sit in on the meeting.

Each time I made a point, she would either interrupt and refute or insert a critical comment that didn't even relate to the topic raised.

Yes, she came intending to hijack the meeting and rattle me.

And she won.

So unaccustomed to such rude behavior and with no tools to get the meeting back on track, I wrapped up quickly and spent the rest of the day damage-controlling and strengthening the team through one-on-one conversations.

Isn't it surprising when people act completely differently than *we* would in a situation?

After that disaster, I intended to learn how to get back to my planned message when disrupted.

That's when I learned the concept of "bridging" to my talking points. As a verbal tactic often used during press conferences, these phrases are not unlike our verbal highlighters mentioned in Day 10 "Serving up a Sound Bite."

Remember, knowing *what* you want to say and reducing the message to simple, clean statements are crucial to being heard.

You've already anticipated pushback that would be reasonable in your situation.

Bridging comes into play when unreasonable or surprise tactics are used intentionally to rattle you.

First, know your talking points like the back of your hand. Then, keep these phrases in your back pocket.

- I *can't* speak to that, but I *can* say this...

- An interesting comment, but let me put this into perspective...

- Here's something equally important to consider...

- It's easy to lose sight of the matter at hand. The real issue is...

- I hear your point; however, our focus is...

"Bridging comes into play when unreasonable or surprise tactics are used intentionally to rattle you."

Words alone won't work. Yes, they should be delivered firmly but also with grace. If you appear flustered, annoyed, or like you are trying to put the distractor in their place, you won't win friends or influence people.

Warning: The next time you observe a press conference or watch a political interview, you may see these tactics *overused*. When someone *constantly deflects*, they appear defensive, and it's a bad look. And if you never answer ANY question...well, you shouldn't have a press conference at all!

You will also notice that outside of your professional arena, well-meaning (or simply sneaky) teenagers, friends, or others will try to distract you by changing a subject mid-stream—especially if they don't like what you're about to say! It could come in the form of a compliment to disarm you or in the form of a distraction like spilling milk.

If this happens, say thank you (and grab a kitchen towel if you have to). Think to yourself, *Clever move!* and then get right back to the message at hand with a smile that says, "I'm on to you."

Since this is an equal opportunity communication book, it may also be beneficial to observe the ways *you* divert others, whether intentionally or subconsciously.

Do you...

- Finish people's sentences, robbing them of the satisfaction of making a point?

- Bring up unrelated offenses when someone wants to address a problem?

- Play with your phone or act visibly unengaged when spoken to?

These passive-aggressive behaviors speak louder than any words. They say, "You will not get through to me."

Bridging is a soft turn to avoid confrontation.

Breathe deeply and use a bridge to cross those troubled waters.

HOW TO BE HEARD
EXERCISE

Notice when someone intentionally tries to change the subject. Ironically, they may often precede this hijacking by saying, "Not to change the subject..." Use a bridging phrase to get back on point.

DAY 20

When You Blow It

"You're flawed. But you're awesome. You're flawsome!
Embrace your flawsomeness.™"

— Brenda Viola

My sister[14] is one of the best calligraphers in the world.

People who plan parties for celebrities, royalty, or billionaires hire her to make their invitations and envelopes distinctively beautiful. Her artistry adorns my apartment (lucky me!) and getting snail mail from her makes my day because it's far more beautiful than anything else in my mailbox.

To emphasize the elite nature of her work, she is required to sign nondisclosure agreements. After all, when you're privy to a movie star's address, inquiring minds want to know! "Invited by whom?" "With a guest?" "Date and time?"

So when a relative asked her to personalize a birthday cookie, she readily agreed, thinking, *I've got this.*

Epic. Fail.

---

[14] You can be inspired by my sister's art @foxyscribe on Instagram!

"It is not perfection that creates connection. In the messy moments, you can win over your audience by being comfortable with yourself."

In her words, "It was as if they had hired a kindergartener to ice 'Happy Birthday' on top!"

A messy mess of an attempt.

And we both laughed at the irony. Luckily, so did the party-goers!

Another epic fail was when I was in the middle of a rousing workshop based on my first book, *The Public Servants' Survival Guide*, and the heel on my shoe fell off.

I could have either hobbled through the next hour or used the wardrobe malfunction for comic relief and removed both shoes to get on with things. (I chose the latter.)

This book is about being heard, about getting *through*. And I can't stress this enough: it is not perfection that creates connection.

In fact, in the messy moments you can win over your audience by being comfortable with yourself.

Yes, you will fumble a phrase and bungle your PowerPoint. You'll have deer-in-the-headlights moments and lose your place. Once, so passionate in my delivery, I nearly fell off a stage.

You will not be perfect.

What you do *next* determines how people remember you and your message.

First of all, please stop apologizing. More than once is too much, and instead of saying, "I'm so sorry I'm late..." say, "Thank you for your patience."

What the audience doesn't know won't hurt you!

If slides 13 through 15 are somehow missing, keep going. If the handouts never got handed out, encourage them to take notes.

And if your luggage...

Oh, this one is near and dear to my heart. I have never missed a speaking engagement and always plan my flights to arrive at least 24 hours before I take the stage.

My flight from Sarasota, Florida, to Jackson, Mississippi, required a layover in Chicago. The first leg went off without a hitch.

As I departed the aircraft in Chicago, murmurs of delays and cancellations surrounded me. As I approached my gate, I saw the dreaded word "DELAYED." Though the agent reassured me that it was only a delay, after two hours, the red letters changed to "CANCELED."

And no other flights to Jackson on that carrier were scheduled until the morning, which was too late.

A disaster.

The agent saw my look of distress and furiously clicked on her computer. "There's a flight boarding right now, but it's four terminals over. If you start running now, you might make it."

You never saw me run so fast. (I probably haven't since then!)

Running through four terminals is no joke. By the time I arrived, heaving and sweaty, they were about to close the flight. But I made it! Sweet relief!

Only to remember that all I had was my laptop and wallet. Everything else remained in a suitcase spending the night at O'Hare.

No contact lenses. No makeup. No clothes.

Oh, I'd make my morning speech, but I'd be in jeans, sneakers, and last night's hair and makeup. (All the drugstores had closed for the night.)

Part of me wanted to just wave the white flag and cancel, but I hadn't come this far to come just this far.

A mistake would have been to spend the first 10 minutes apologizing for my appearance. Instead, I spoke with passion about the resilience of the human spirit and how it rises when we face everyday challenges. I didn't apologize for my imperfect appearance; I embraced it.

In some ways, I think my mess helped my message land. Because who can relate to an imperfect person?

Everyone.

That lisp...or extra 30 pounds...or lack of a degree. What you have to say matters far more than any of these perceived inadequacies.

Truly, it's not just external mishaps that shut us up. Far more often, it's the internal critic that screams, "Who do you think you *are*?"

Too many people never speak up, apply for a better job, or ask that person out on a date because they are ever aware of their imperfections.

They talk themselves out of trying rather than risk failing.

Perfectionism is the birthplace of imposter syndrome.

We'll get into what's fueling this perfectionism in the next chapter. But in the meantime, make my phrase your mantra: Embrace Your Flawsomeness!™

HOW TO BE HEARD
EXERCISE

What flaws or imperfections cause you to disqualify yourself? Silence that inner critic and seek an opportunity to speak up when you would normally shut down.

"Who can relate to an imperfect person? Everyone."

DAY 21

Making Peace with Fear

"Do the thing you fear to do and keep on doing it…
that is the quickest and surest way ever
yet discovered to conquer fear."

— Dale Carnegie

Sixteen wasn't sweet for me.

The popular girls in my small high school collectively decided they no longer liked me. Worse, they actively hated me.

From chewed gum wrapped around my locker to threatening notes left on my car, I detoured from certain hallways to escape their wrath and felt if I could just be invisible, I'd survive another day.

As I mentioned briefly in the introduction, engrained in my memory is an encounter so vivid that recalling it over 40 years later makes me shudder. As I turned a corner to go up a stairwell, a group of 20 surrounded me. And together, they began barking.

Barking!

"Fear is a fact of life,
so make peace with it."

I kept my head down and kept moving forward, tears stinging my eyes. So gripped by rejection and braced for the daily onslaught, my grades plummeted. No more extracurricular activities or football games for me. I let fear rob me of my remaining high school years and never once considered standing up for myself.

The greatest fear was that they were right! That there was something fundamentally wrong with me.

It took me decades to realize that what *was* wrong was being surprised by the presence of fear! Fearless living is impossible. It's how you respond to it that will either make you or break you.

Succumb to it, and you will shrink. Face it, and you will grow.

Fear is a fact of life, so make peace with it.

One of my all-time favorite movies is *Defending Your Life* starring Albert Brooks and Meryl Streep. You'll chuckle at the early '90s references and laugh at the plot. But the premise compels me to watch this film over and over again.

The main characters meet in the afterlife after suffering untimely deaths. In a "holding area" prior to judgment day, they develop a bond. Along the way, they learn that it's not good deeds or church attendance that win them the golden ticket to Heaven. It's how they did—or didn't—face their fears.

I won't give away the ending, but you'll love it (and you'll root heartily for Daniel Miller).

When it comes to speaking, either on stage before thousands or in an important conversation with someone I love, I still feel fear.

And do it anyway.

My work with Vici Communications LLC[15] includes coaching professionals who want to fine-tune presentations or excel when interviewed by the media or a podcaster. A recent client shared: "This opportunity is so important, and I'm so scared."

Understandable!

I responded, "But aren't you also *excited*?"

She nodded.

Fear and excitement feel alike. The difference? Energy.

Fear is a negative energy fueled by anxious thoughts and ruminations. "What if I say something wrong?" "What if they hate me?" "What if I trip or choke or forget my talking points?" "What if I'm a fraud and shouldn't even be speaking at all?"

Every nightmare begins with the words "What if…"

However, so does every dream come true.

Excitement is positive energy fueled by hopeful possibilities. "What if my message effects change?" "What if new clients come from this interview?" "What if I feel great because I spoke my truth?"

You get to choose your "What if's…"

---

[15] As a recovering fraidy-cat who let the bullies win for far too long, this chapter means a great deal to me. That's why I named my company Vici Communications LLC instead of Viola. "Vici" means "I conquered," and I wear the very act of starting a brand-new life at 60 years old as my badge of honor. I conquered stuff to get here! And I live to help people conquer their stuff, too.

And when, in the history of worrying, did it ever help? Do you know anyone who has ever said, "Gosh, I'm so glad I stayed up all night worrying about *that!*"

If it would help, I'd say go for it! But all fear wants you to do is shut up and shut down.

Don't let the bully win.

So what are some practical ways to make peace with fear?

I'm a huge proponent of encouragement. At the very heart of the word is "courage," and boy, don't we need *that* to speak up when it's scary?

Who are your go-to people, the ones who will lift you up and cheer you on? Get them involved. Visualize the scenario going exactly as you would hope. Imagine speaking the words and watching them land.

Remember, the more prepared you are, the less scared you are.

Yes, you'll still have butterflies because you're human. But don't beat yourself up for that!

When we try to ignore the fear or pretend it isn't there, it creates a disconnect that will not serve your message.

I also caution against fighting the fear because it'll wear you out, like trying to dislodge sticky tape from your fingers. Acknowledge it. Reframe it as excitement when possible. Gulp and move forward.

Another way I nudge myself away from voting with fear is to ask this question, "Will I regret *not* speaking up?" If the answer is yes, it's a tipping point to feel the fear...and do it anyway.

James Neil Hollingworth said it best: "Courage is not the absence of fear, but rather the assessment that something else is more important than fear."

What you have to say is important. And only you can say it. Stop making yourself miserable by putting it off.

Just like the Cowardly Lion had bravery[16] all along, so do you. Use it!

HOW TO BE HEARD
E X E R C I S E

Identify a situation that needs to be addressed but you've been too afraid to speak up. Practice some positive "What if's" and rally some trusted encouragers to support you. Acknowledge the fear but feed the part of you that senses the irresistible must. Obey that…and at least you won't live with the regret of never having tried.

---

[16] I'm a fan of playing some good music to pump yourself up. A perfect choice when feeling afraid of speaking up? "Brave" by Sara Bareilles. Turn those speakers up!

"Every nightmare begins with the words 'What if...' However, so does every dream come true."

DAY 22

The Method Matters

"The odds of hitting your target go up dramatically
when you aim for it."

— Mal Pancoast

When I served as a public information officer, the world began to change. Instead of waiting for the weekly paper to report the news, we embraced technology that would allow us to convey important information to our community. A press release covering the who, what, when, where, why, and how would be posted on the township's website, scripted into government access TV shows, read at public meetings, included in the township newsletter, and emailed to citizen bloggers and community groups.

Talk about overcommunicating! You'd think we covered all the bases, right?

Officials spoke publicly for *months* about a new recycling program, but when distribution of the new bins began in the first of many neighborhoods, residents were outraged. "Where's my old bin?" "How much of my taxpayer dollars were spent on this?" The municipal building's phone lines were ablaze with complaints.

"Your message can be spot on, but if you're not using the right method, it's going to fall flat."

Clearly, our communication methods hadn't hit the mark.

We paused the program to come up with a solution. Our brilliant manager said, "Let's stick flyers on the *old* bins."

On recycling day, our public works crews were equipped with 15,000 bright yellow flyers (printed on recyclable paper, of course). When each household retrieved their bin from the curbside, the message was unavoidable. "Thank you for recycling! Effective September 1, this bin will be retrieved and replaced with a brand-new container. No taxpayer funds were spent to upgrade your bins. A state grant has fully funded this program."

The point of this story? Yes, use all the traditional methods at your disposal, but don't forget what works for your audience. Every member of this audience had an existing recycling container, so that's where the message was best planted.

One of my favorite charitable events to support is The Main Line Chamber Foundation's Scholarship Program for volunteer firefighters. An annual 5K run brings the community together and generates thousands—over $70,000 in 2023 alone—to support the educational pursuits of hometown heroes.

Each June, elected officials, local dignitaries, the 17 fire companies serving the Main Line area, and the public are invited to the scholarship ceremony. Letters are mailed to each firefighter, inviting them to publicly receive their award. The local paper prints their names; follow-up phone calls are made.

When it was my job to ensure attendance, just 10% of the firefighters were RSVP'd a week before the ceremony!

Hmmmmm. I thought collecting a check would be enough of an incentive to show up.

Panicked at the thought of a packed auditorium but only a smattering of firefighters, I remembered the demographic with whom I wanted to communicate.

Snail mail? C'mon! What were you *thinking*, Brenda?

These 18-year-olds were tethered to their phones...and I had their cell numbers.

Within an hour, I received every RSVP via text.

Your message can be spot on, but if you're not using the right method, it's going to fall flat.

A great way to navigate this potential pitfall is to simply ask.

My public service professional life emphasized the written word. My manager preferred his team to email him about issues, requests, and ideas.

After a decade and thousands of written words, I accepted a position in the private sector. And continued to produce all of my communication using email.

And never received a response.

The nerve!

No one EVER got back to me, and when asked questions I found myself repeating, "I put that in an email to all of you last Thursday..."

My frustration grew until I finally asked my new employer,

"Why don't you answer my emails?"

He looked perplexed. "Brenda, I hate email."

Aargh!

But *he* wasn't wrong. *I* was wrong for assuming that his preferred method of communication was the same as my former boss's. Turns out, he favored a phone call or face-to-face. Once I pivoted, I couldn't have asked for a more responsive, engaged leader.

If your communication is landing in a void, consider that the method you are using needs to change.

HOW TO BE HEARD
E X E R C I S E

Think about the people you communicate with most often. Have you ever asked them if they prefer email, text, a phone call, or face-to-face exchanges? Pick the person who most frustrates you by their lack of response and ask. You might be surprised by the answer (and it could make things much better).

DAY 23

Make Your Messes
Your Message

"Grace means that all of your mistakes now serve
a purpose instead of serving shame."

— **Sherianna Boyle**

Just a few of my messes include...

Sinking into freshly poured concrete on my first day on the job as a public servant.

A live wireless microphone amplifying that pre-meeting trip to the bathroom.

Missing the last ferry out of Martha's Vineyard when chaperoning a high school class and spending the night at the ferry station.

A can of cling peaches exploding live on-air when I was a *QVC* show host. (Or being assigned to sell Craftsman tools when I didn't know a socket from a ratchet. Now *that* was one agonizing hour!)

An engaging, funny story brings much-needed levity to learning. What once made you wince is bait that captures your audience's attention. Being able to laugh at yourself is speaking gold! When the person listening is laughing, the soil for the seeds you're planting is fertilized.

Then, there are weightier topics that are more difficult to share.

A marriage ended.

A partner's sudden death.

Unresolved issues with aging parents (or caretaking challenges).

The sting of a missed opportunity.

The regret of not standing up for the underdog.

We've all got messes in our lives. There's not one person on Earth who is flawless (refer to Day 20, "When You Blow It"). Every success story is paved with a host of failures, but imperfections should never disqualify you from speaking up. Instead, they often break down barriers to being heard.

The best communicators have made peace with their downfalls and use the lessons learned to help others.

Do you want your listener to open their mind—and, more importantly, their heart—to you?

Then *you* go first.

I'm not suggesting that you indiscriminately wear your heart on your sleeve. But being willing to reveal your heart can create a connection that no number of facts and figures could achieve.

"An engaging, funny story brings much-needed levity to learning."

Be intentional about what you share. Sharing your messes shouldn't be about evoking sympathy. The goals are to...

- Create connection ("We share common challenges...")

- Highlight tools ("Here's how I addressed the situation...")

- Amplify the lesson ("On the other side of this, I learned...")

Sure, you could create a five-point outline, but everyone will forget it. Immediately.

But if you tell your story? They'll not only remember it, they'll also likely tell others, reinforcing the very points you made and solidifying your message in their minds.

Here's the best benefit of sharing your messes with candor: It frees the listener up to accept their *own* messes (or to at least consider making peace with their past).

You provide a living, breathing example of how your story *didn't* end after screwing up or missing the boat.

Do any of you remember a TV series from the '80s called *Thirtysomething*? In one scene, a lead actor played by Ken Olin ruminates over a missed opportunity. He is so agitated that he can't sleep and sits on the couch, channel-surfing for hours.

And he has an "Aha!" moment.

Hours before, an item on a shopping channel was presented as "your last chance," but when he landed there again, the same offer reappeared! His conclusion: there's always another chance.

I'll never forget that scene, because many times in my own life I thought, *Stick a fork in me. I'm done.*

Each time, instead of breaking me, the perceived failure ended up making me.

And the lessons learned? Priceless.

To this day, they play a starring role in important conversations, coaching calls, or speaking engagements.

Yes, sometimes my throat catches and I need to take a beat to collect myself. But showing authentic emotion always enhances the words spoken.

Most people are rooting for you, not judging you. So don't judge yourself.

The things that go wrong are often the brightest colors in the tapestry of your life.

And they can be a beacon of hope to other imperfect people, just like me and you.

HOW TO BE HEARD
EXERCISE

Are there mistakes from the past that haunt your present? Can you make peace with your imperfections and even use them to help another person? Owning your stories and sharing them will increase your impact substantially. Perhaps more importantly, accepting your mistakes and embracing the lessons learned can contribute to healing old wounds.

"The things that go wrong are often the brightest colors in the tapestry of your life."

DAY 24

And the Hero Is…

"A person with heroes is more likely to become a hero."

— **Anonymous**

At every chance he got, Eric would authentically praise someone.

A successful company president, he had plenty of reasons to toot his own horn. Instead, each time a compliment came his way, he'd deflect the spotlight and place it on a member of his team.

When speaking at all-hands-on-deck meetings, he relished shouting out employees by name. And none of it was fake. He truly enjoyed acknowledging others.

He was one of my all-time favorite colleagues, and to this day he'll send me a text noticing a recent accomplishment or sharing a kind word overheard about me in a meeting.

Everybody loves Eric. Because *he's* not the hero of his own stories.

And as a result, he is a hero to many people.

Yes, share your stories to create connection, but never forget to turn the spotlight on others wherever possible.

A concept mentioned way back on Day 2 of this book bears repeating. The master at winning friends and influencing people, Dale Carnegie, famously taught: "A person's name is, to that person, the sweetest and most important sound in any language."

You want to be heard? Without screaming?

Use a person's name.

"Not being the hero of the stories you tell" is a concept I first learned at a sales training meeting almost a decade ago. Presented by organizational psychologist Ryan Avery,[17] the idea was profoundly simple and nudged my conscience each time I was tempted to play the starring role in a presentation.

If it's all about you, there's no room for *them*.

People love to listen to big-hearted people who aren't attention hogs.

Here's the remarkable thing about attention: If you need it, crave it, or demand it…it will be elusive. You'll continually be irritated by the praise showered on others and wonder why no one is noticing your amazingness. All that posturing is exhausting!

---

[17] Ryan Avery is a renowned keynote speaker and author of one of my favorite books on communication: *Speaker, Leader, Champion*. When I met him, what fascinated me most was that he beat out 30,000 other people to become Toastmasters' 2012 World Public Speaking Champion (and at the time, the youngest in history).

"Amplifying what's good in other people brings out the best in you."

I know. (Recovering attention addict here.)

Settling my own worth[18] released me from the constant need to prove myself. Instead of clamoring to make my presence known, it freed me up to "just be." And remarkably, my desire to make *others* the hero grew.

Now *I'm* a deflector. It's delightful to shine the light on someone else, whether a colleague, audience member, restaurant server, or relative.

Amplifying what's good in other people brings out the best in you.

HOW TO BE HEARD
EXERCISE

Bite your tongue the next time you're tempted to be the star of a story! Instead, consider the many others who often play supporting roles—and give them the spotlight. Use their names, cite specifics about their accomplishments, point them out in a group setting, and watch how they blossom from the positive attention.

---

[18] The keynote entitled "Settle Your Worth to Launch a Better Life" is perhaps my most popular speech. Too many people settle for less in their personal and professional lives because they haven't yet made peace with their own worthiness.

DAY 25

The Golden Rule

"When you rearrange the word LISTEN, you end up with SILENT.
Are you really listening?"

— Freddie Ravel

We were 30 minutes into the first date, and he hadn't stopped talking. Hardly took a breath. Nor had he even asked me one question! I thought, *How can I possibly extract myself from this excruciating situation without being rude?*

When he took a beat to sip his cocktail, I said, "Do you have anything *you'd* like to ask *me*?"

He sputtered. "Oh, I guess I've been doing most of the talking…"

But he still didn't pick up on the hint. And the night ended early. (The headache was real, though!)

Communication should be a cha-cha—a back-and-forth dance that picks up on and follows threads of information. The only way a good conversation works is if you spend half of the time listening.

Really listening.

"The only way a good conversation works is if you spend half of the time listening."

Not thinking of the next thing you're going to say but being present and engaged. This is an art learned through practice. You'll find yourself reigning in your monkey mind[19] over and over until you achieve full engagement. It's crucial to master this.

People want to feel seen. And heard.

Darting eyes scanning the room say, "Hey, you're not all that interesting, and I'm looking for someone better to jump to…"

I know, you might be thinking, "But that person is soooooooo boring!"

Well, if you never ask a question, so are you.

When not consumed by your own thoughts, you have capacity for the ideas and stories of others.

Think about one of the first examples in this book. Dr. Judy D'Angelo (Day 2: "The Waiting Game") won over everyone in the room because she not only let everyone else speak first, she also took notes on what they said and quoted them when it was her turn!

Of *course* everyone wanted to listen to her!

So how can you demonstrate that you've truly listened? We've already established that being curious and asking questions is a great way to engage.

---

[19] The term "monkey mind" is rooted in Buddhist teachings and describes a state where one's mind is restless, capricious, whimsical, and uncontrollable.

In both personal and professional settings, simply repeating or paraphrasing what you heard is effective. "What I think I heard you say..." is also helpful to clear up confusion and gives the person a chance to adjust or correct any misconceptions.

A method my friend Kevin uses is to follow up a day later with either a text or a phone call.

"You know...I've been thinking about what you said..."

What a compliment!

Not only did he listen, he's also been thinking about it and wants to take it further. Because he listens so well, my ears are perked up when *he* has something to say.

It's the Golden Rule. If you want someone to hear *you*, give *them* the gift of your undivided attention.

HOW TO BE HEARD
E X E R C I S E

Shock someone by being fully engaged when they talk. Maintain eye contact, nod, ask questions, and repeat what you've heard. Observe how it makes you both feel.

DAY 26

Don't Say It!

"Even fools are thought wise if they keep silent,
and discerning if they hold their tongues."

— Proverbs 17:28 (NIV)

"Wait a minute!"

(I can hear you.)

"You've just spent the past 25 chapters encouraging me to speak UP, and now you're suggesting I should be QUIET?"

Not all the time.

But when it is burning on your tongue and you feel as if your head will pop off if you don't say something, that's the time to zip it.

Why?

Because what you say is so inflamed with emotion, the validity of your point is likely to be lost. If you're that fired up, you need to first cool down, or you'll say something you regret.

One of my very happy places is in Zumba® class. Not since my heyday of '80s clubbing have I enjoyed the freedom of dancing with abandon and working up a healthy sweat. Antonio is one of my instructors at Life Time in La Jolla, California, and his energy evokes whoops, hollers, clapping, and shimmying. For me, it's pure bliss.

We reserve assigned spots on the floor via the Life Time app so we each have room to shake what our mommas gave us.

Then SHE showed up.

Completely oblivious to those around her, she almost bumped into me several times, flailing her arms widely, veering off to dance in MY reserved spot, and...

...I wanted to knock her block off.

Seriously, it took everything in me to not forcibly shove her off of spot number 20!

I bit my tongue.

This was *her* happy place, too, after all.

I resolved, mid-shimmy, to shake it off and just focus on my samba.

As if some energetic force field had lifted, she suddenly turned to me and said, "I'm so sorry! I was so caught up in trying not to miss a step, I drifted into your spot!"

Crisis averted!

If I'd voted with the devil over my shoulder, a spat would have ensued, making all future Zumba® classes uncomfortable. (She was also a regular.) How glad I am that I controlled myself!

But oh, how I wish that was *always* the case!

My rearview includes a few outbursts, knee-jerk reactions, and emotion-inflamed conversations fueled by my inability to simply wait.

Such outbursts diminish my credibility.

And people will dismiss your valid points if they are packaged too emotionally.

Here are six useful questions to help you determine when *not* to speak up:

- Are you able to give the other person the benefit of the doubt?

- Can you be curious rather than judgmental about the perceived slight?

- Will the words spoken potentially burn a bridge?

- Have you given considerable thought to how to approach the subject?

- Are you calm?

- Does it absolutely, positively need to be addressed right now?

Sometimes bridges DO need to be burned. And there *are* rascals who don't deserve the benefit of the doubt, considering their past behavior.

However, according to a Sierra Leonian proverb, "Quarrels end. But words, once spoken, never die."

Gulping down salty words can, in the moment, feel like swallowing seawater. But the best time to speak is after the initial sting has passed.

Exercising restraint keeps you from being branded a blowhard and legitimizes the times when you do need to assert yourself.

HOW TO BE HEARD
EXERCISE

You know your triggers. Whether it's that slow driver in the left lane or your mother-in-law at Thanksgiving dinner, use restraint. Sense what's happening in your body as you gulp down that retort. Breathe. Then applaud yourself for exercising this important skill.

"The best time to speak is after the initial sting has passed."

DAY 27

Ask For What You Want

"You get in life what you have the courage to ask for."

— Oprah Winfrey

You know those five love languages? (If not, learn about them at 5lovelanguages.com.)

I like them all, of course, but without shame I confess: Presents do it for me. Give me a pretty package wrapped with a sparkly bow, and I almost don't care what's inside. It just thrills me to have a package to open.

Or an envelope! Mark knew that one of my favorite daily highlights was checking the mailbox to see if "presents" were delivered. Sure, there were far more catalogs and bills than fun mail, but I was still delighted to see what might show up on any given day.

Which is why my first Christmas as a married woman was such a disaster.

I had written a poem and wrapped a half-dozen special things I knew he would love.

"So much energy is wasted and negative emotion fueled when we assume and don't ask for what we really want."

He presented me with one box, haphazardly wrapped and filled with rocks (to throw me off) with a gift card enclosed.

I burst into tears. He was horrified, clueless about what crime he'd committed.

Clearly, the art of being heard without screaming wasn't yet something I had mastered.

The truth? I expected him to read my mind and gift the way *I* gifted.[20]

My internal critic screamed, "How could you live with me for an entire year and not have a clue what kind of present I'd like?"[21]

So much energy is wasted and negative emotion fueled when we assume and don't ask for what we really want.

In big and small ways, being clear about what you want and asking for it will serve you.

For example, back when I was less adept at managing my finances, I was shocked to learn that overdraft or late fees could be removed if I simply ASKED.

Or how about this one? Before remote work was commonplace, I resigned from a job I loved because my husband wanted to

---

[20] The book *The Four Agreements* was referenced back on Day 7 "Read the Room (but Don't Take it Personally)." Aside from not taking things personally, the other three agreements are "Do your best," "Be impeccable with your word," and the one I failed at miserably in my marriage, "Don't make assumptions." I find that when I'm "off" or troubled, it's usually because I violated one of the four.

[21] I'm sure there are plenty of spouses who would be thrilled to receive a gift card. I'm just not one of them.

move to Florida. It never occurred to me to ask to stay and work from home, because it hadn't been done before!

Imagine how glad (and relieved) I was when my employer asked me, "Do you think you could do your job from Florida?"

"Yes! A million times yes!"

A fruitful decade followed that included some of my most creative work and successful employee engagement programs that remain in place to this day.

So what are you lacking or allowing to frustrate you because you never asked for what you really want?

Of course, not every ask will be responded to with a "yes." But "no's" help clarify the best next steps for you.

When you think of regrets, they more likely involve the things you wanted that you never pursued. (That prom date? Or promotion?)

Take the leap!

HOW TO BE HEARD
EXERCISE

What is something you want that you have never acted on because you were afraid to ask? This "something" takes up residence in your heart and mind, and you often ruminate over it. Hone your message, anticipate pushback, and choose your timing. Then ask for what you want!

DAY 28

Those Difficult Conversations

"The courageous conversation is the one you don't want to have."

— David Whyte

You may have fully mastered the art of gulping down salty words!

While such restraint can absolutely serve you, sometimes you set yourself up for an explosion when you continually delay a difficult conversation.

You've been stung again and again, and swallowed your retorts successfully.

But your buttons continue to be pushed. And the slow burn is headed to a boil.

I'm not saying it'll be easy, but you *need* to address it, or you *will* lose it.

It takes courage to clear the air, and life becomes increasingly uncomfortable to live through the static of unresolve.

Lisa and Judy[22] became besties in kindergarten. Matching pencil boxes (remember them?), surviving middle school angst, and full-blown high school ups and downs were navigated as a team until their paths diverged.

When Lisa went to college and Judy got married, they remained close. Each held their long-term relationship as a badge of honor.

Then Lisa married a loser, and Judy's husband evolved into a wildly successful entrepreneur.

Judy had never been enamored with the trappings of success, so it didn't change her.

But Lisa?

Her jealousy festered for *decades*. Though not blatant, she aimed nasty jabs toward Judy.

Judy found herself distancing from the relationship, dreading dates on the calendar, and bracing herself for the next passive-aggressive exchange.

This friendship of half a century headed toward an explosion because as nice as Judy was, she found her headspace con-sumed with a full-blown confrontation when *not* in Lisa's presence.

Conflict isn't fun, but dreading conflict will drain your energy and distract you from all the other happy parts of your life.

Judy wisely wrote out her thoughts to clear her mind.

---

[22] Names and certain details have been changed to protect privacy.

"Dreading conflict will drain your energy and distract you from all the other happy parts of your life."

Then, she picked up the phone.

Careful to not put Lisa on the defensive, she asked if it was a good time, and when Lisa said yes, she said, "I'd like us to talk through some static I'm feeling in our relationship..."

I'd love to say "...and they lived happily ever after."

Instead, Lisa exploded, unleashing a tirade of venom she'd bottled up for years. It became clear there would be no path forward.

Actually, that *is* a happy ending.

We too often stay in toxic relationships because of the time already invested.

But does it make sense to spend *more* time on a sinking ship?

And if the ship *is* sinking, that's an important conversation to have!

A coach I once worked with explained how to have "clearing conversations." A key to this approach working is relinquishing the need to be (or feel) "right," so bear that in mind before proceeding.

Here's my paraphrased version, but you can discover many different variations on this theme:

1. **Present the conversation.** "Can we set up a time to talk? I'd like us to work through something because this relationship (personally or professionally) is important to me."

2. **Share the facts.** These are the unarguable details, followed by what feelings followed and how you have interpreted the situation.

3. **Seek to understand.** "I'd like to know your thoughts about this and whether you can see or disagree with my take on it." You could really learn something here about how you've misinterpreted or overreacted. Perhaps you'll discover why they said or acted in a way that created static between you.

4. **Present a path forward.** You may agree to disagree, but a great outcome is to do so respectfully. You can hopefully learn more about each other and discover more effective ways to communicate that don't fuel divisiveness.

A clearing should make both parties feel better and less likely to combust.

Yes, you may still have to burn that bridge, but when you do it calmly, thoughtfully, and from a place of peace, you're not as likely to serve up a plate of regret afterward.

The fact is, you're not going to like everyone.

And they're not going to like you. (Shocking! I know.)

You can't always make peace with the other person, but never sacrifice being at peace with yourself.

Try to achieve *that* before having an uncomfortable conversation.

HOW TO BE HEARD
EXERCISE

Is there a conversation you've been delaying because it's not something you're looking forward to? Walk through the clearing process by yourself first, and then take the courageous step of asking for a clearing.

DAY 29

The (Not So) Secret Ingredient

"Love never fails."

— I Corinthians 13:8 (NIV)

One of my favorite spots in Siesta Key Village in Florida debuted on *Shark Tank* in 2013. Sub Zero Nitrogen Ice Cream was (and is) delicious. But watching the team zap ingredients with liquid nitrogen to create custom, decadent ice-cream desserts was downright entertaining.

The combination of ingredients is limited only by your imagination.

However, amidst the coconut, fresh fruit, chocolate, marshmallows, gummies, and a host of other treats was one silver shaker bottle.

It was labeled "LOVE."

(I always asked for liberal doses.)

Everything tastes better when you feel the love blended into it.

Each year, to honor my grandmother, Edna Hartsell, I bake her famous raisin bread and ship close to 30 loaves throughout the

"Everything sounds better when your audience can feel the love in your message."

country. I always insert a holiday note and tell everyone, "There's lots of love baked in each loaf." And there really is.

When it comes to your communication, Carl Buehner's quote referenced earlier in this book should be a guiding principle: "I've learned that people will forget what you said, people will forget what you did, but people will never forget how you made them feel."

Everything sounds better when your audience can feel the love in your message.

Oh, you may not have something warm or fuzzy to say, but it can still be marinated in love.

Love—don't dread—your audience. (They'll feel it.)

So how do you love your audience?

If we look at the "love never fails" passage in I Corinthians 13, it is preceded by the qualities, or fruits, of love. Here's a break-down from the Revised Standard Version (RSV): *Love is patient and kind; love is not jealous or boastful; it is not arrogant or rude. Love does not insist on its own way; it is not irritable or resentful; it does not rejoice at wrong but rejoices in the right. Love bears all things, believes all things, hopes all things, endures all things.*

These qualities each play a role in the preceding chapters.

But here's an important note: don't forget to apply them to *yourself.*

Love—don't judge—yourself. (You'll feel it.)

Will you always say things the right way? Nope. And when you don't, learn from it, apologize, and then forgive yourself.

You'll be impatient, unkind, jealous, and boastful. You'll occasionally be arrogant and manipulate to get your own way because...you're human. (Refer to the aforementioned "flawsome.")

Irritable? Absolutely. And you'll want to throw in the towel instead of "bearing all things."

That's when you can flip back to "When You Blow It" (Day 20) and "Make Your Messes Your Message" (Day 23).

You will fail at love.

But love will never fail you.

Like a flowing river that never runs dry, it's at the very core of who you are. In my own life, I've found that even when I feel all dried up, saying, "Help me tap into the love..." causes miraculous springs to trickle forth.

My personal prayer, each time I take the stage or have a meeting—even when I'm sitting for a manicure or shimmying in Zumba® class—is "Let each person I meet today encounter love through me."

Even on tough days, that prayer has never failed.

Remember, that's *not* where I started! I'm the one who jockeyed for position in every scenario, seeking to hog the spotlight.

A series of losses from 2021 to 2023 dislodged me from life as I knew it. Suddenly, all those days and nights spent glued to a computer screen striving for success instead of being present with the people dearest to me seemed a waste.

"Love in such a way that every person you meet can feel it."

With my faulty ideas of a "successful" life stripped away, there was nothing left to live for.

Except love.

To give and receive it.

Everything else, as the old Carole King song says, "... is illusion."[23]

Mastering love[24] is a lifelong pursuit, but a worthy one.

When you master love, there's nothing you *can't* say (and you may find new restraint when speaking at all!).

A warm smile can take the place of a multitude of words, and it works like a magnet, drawing people to you and your message.

There's a famous, anonymous quote that goes like this: "Speak in such a way that others love to listen to you. Listen in such a way that others love to speak to you."

But I'd add one other sentence:

"Love in such a way that every person you meet can feel it."

---

[23] "Only Love Is Real" is a song written and performed by Carole King. The song was included on her 1976 album, Thoroughbred. Though one of her lesser-known hits, the lyrics speak timeless truth. Look it up and have a listen!

[24] *The Mastery of Love* is another wonderful book by Don Miguel Ruiz. Here's one beautiful quote from it: "Happiness can only come from inside of you and is the result of your love. When you are aware that no one else can make you happy, and that happiness is the result of your love, this becomes the greatest mastery of the Toltec: the Mastery of Love."

Your responsibilities as a speaker are to be prepared and clear about the message you need to convey. But first? Be rooted and grounded in love (not fear).

Love makes everyone feel safe and comfortable.

Whether it's a crowd or your kid, when others sense your genuine love, it opens their hearts and minds to hear you.

No screaming is necessary.

HOW TO BE HEARD
E X E R C I S E

Test-drive the prayer "Let each person I meet today encounter love through me." See what happens!

DAY 30

Lean In

"Woman need to shift from thinking 'I'm not ready to do that' to thinking 'I want to do that—and I'll learn by doing it.'"

— Sheryl Sandburg

My employer sent me to crisis communication school, and I sat in a room surrounded by public relations pros and information officers whose jobs were far bigger than my own.

Over the course of six hours, we learned some of the techniques described in this book, like "bridging" (Day 19). Attending mock press conferences, crafting press releases, and wordsmithing sound bites filled the day, which was nirvana for a word nerd like me!

At the very end, they asked for one volunteer to use all the skills taught in a role-playing TV interview.

I really wanted to raise my hand.

To my surprise, half of the class volunteered me! (What an honor.)

"Start saying yes to opportunities to speak, and along the way, you'll find your voice."

The *other* half of the class wanted Eric, a very polished public relations pro who worked for a public utility, to represent the class.

So we voted.

Intimidated and insecure, I didn't vote for myself.

And I lost by one vote.

Mind you, it was a small blip in my career as a communicator, but I'll never forget the disappointment of not being brave enough to try.

Start saying yes to opportunities to speak, and along the way, you'll find your voice.

Practicing the tips presented from the previous 29 days will help you use it skillfully.

Don't talk yourself out of speaking.

Yes, someone else might say it differently...but no one can say it like *you*. No one else has your stories! Or your personality, unique frame of reference, tone of voice, or style.

You've got something to say, and when you lean into the opportunity, doors previously closed to you will open. You'll unleash power that, like the lion's courage, was there all along. When you obey that prompting, it will feel so good!

Perhaps even more impactful? When it's not the right time or you're unclear on what should be said, you'll remain silent until clarity comes.

Like any muscle, you've got to exercise to strengthen your communication skills.

After 59 years of resisting all forms of physical exertion, I had an awakening. This body is the only one I've got, and I'm either going to be in training for a good quality of life or be feeble.

Taking baby steps, I first started to sauna. Then I took a Zumba® class. Followed by strength training.

At age 60, I am officially a gym rat. A beast! I throw down kettlebells!

I love feeling strong. Who knew exercise could be fun? (Many of you, probably.)

A wise person once told me, "Before you can change anything in your life, you've got to change your identity."

For many years, I identified as sedentary, uncoordinated, and resistant to sweat.

I had to change my mind before I could change my life.

One baby step after the next changed me forever.

If you used to identify with 75% of the population who are afraid to speak, change your mind.

Exercise the muscle.

Find your voice and use it skillfully.

HOW TO BE HEARD
E X E R C I S E

Volunteer yourself, vote for yourself, or seize an opportunity to speak up. Notice how the more you do, the better it feels.

"Someone else might say it differently…but no one can say it like *you*."

BONUS DAY

"But What About When Someone's Screaming at ME?"

"A soft answer turns away wrath."

— Proverbs 15:1

My favorite spot to drink a latte and people watch in La Jolla is at a café called Queenstown on a busy corner right across from my happy place gym, Life Time on Wall Street. Lemons grow on potted plants, and a puppy dog parade invariably entertains me as I sit, nestled among happy, yellow umbrellas. It's my idea of bliss.

When recently visiting with a friend, a clearly unstable person walked by, stopped, stared directly at me, and screamed, "Eat @#$%!"

Hmmmmmm...

I had done nothing to provoke the insult, but it stung, penetrating my peace for a moment.

Then I breathed a prayer, thankful for the calmness of my mind, and sent love his way.

There was nothing for me to say. You can't argue with madness.

But *had* I taken it personally (thank you, Don Miguel Ruiz), it would have provoked me.

This experience brought back a memory. Some 20 years ago, I meandered through a shopping and dining area in Manayunk, Pennsylvania. My companion at the time was someone I considered to be my closest friend.

As we strolled and shopped, we were abruptly verbally assaulted by a homeless person with similar unstable energy.

He screamed at my friend, "You're a FAKE!"

She exploded.

Her screams exceeded his, and I wondered at the time, *Why is she engaging instead of just letting it roll off of her back?*

Interestingly, I soon learned that she was, in fact, a fake. A liar. A wolf in sheep's clothing and a person unworthy of trust or loyalty.

That's why she screamed back.

His attack touched on a truth she wanted to remain hidden.

When you've got nothing to hide, there's no reason to fight.

When you are at peace with yourself, you can hold your peace.

The two examples previously cited don't apply to all situations because, after all, the screamers were strangers.

What about when it's someone you truly care about?

It's worth repeating this previously shared quote from *Parks and Recreation*'s Leslie Knope (played hilariously by Amy Poehler): "What I hear when I'm being yelled at is people caring loudly at me."

What's behind the raised voice is either...

- Something the person cares deeply about.

- Something the person is deeply afraid of.

Both can be met with compassion and empathy. The worst thing you can do is match their tone.

Just looking at someone I care about with kindness in my eyes can help defuse anger.

Sometimes people just need to vent! (I know I do.)

For those who are overwhelmed and drowning in a sea of emotions, love is a lifeline. But if you go overboard trying to save them, you could end up drowning, too.

Stay in your place of peace, and hopefully, they'll eventually join you.

If you can infuse a smile or humor into what you say (without being disingenuous), I highly recommend doing so!

However, when screaming is the prevalent method of communication, it's a warning light, a cry for help.

Conversely, if you can't speak without crying, this is also a signal for help!

Amplified emotion is usually the overflow of suppressed emotion, and simply applying communication best practices won't make things better.

"Out of the abundance of the heart, the mouth speaks." – Matthew 12:34

In my own life, I have found that such matters of the heart are best navigated with the help of skilled professionals.

HOW TO BE HEARD
EXERCISE

The next time someone yells at you, practice staying in peace. (I always say, "Rest in peace is not just for dead people.") Notice how your calm energy impacts the interaction.

"When you've got nothing to hide, there's no reason to fight. When you are at peace with yourself, you can hold your peace."

Your Next Steps

"What we learn with pleasure we never forget."

— Alfred Mercier

Congratulations on making it through the 30 (well, 31) days of communication exercises! Finding your voice is one of the most powerful shifts you can make in life. Using it skillfully? That takes practice, but life provides an abundance of opportunities to strengthen your communication muscle.

When speaking, my H-E-A-R-D method will help you win the day with five easy-to-remember guidelines:

> H – Have a Plan
> E – Edit Yourself
> A – Anticipate Pushback
> R – Repeat Yourself
> D – Demonstrate That You Listen

As a thank you for reading this book, follow this QR code and use the password **TheHEARDMethod** to gain access to a one-hour video that delves into the H-E-A-R-D method while reinforcing the concepts presented in *How to Be Heard Without Screaming!*

Want to Make Your Next Meeting or Conference Unforgettable?

In 2024, I trademarked the phrase "Aha! moments. Guaranteed."

Why? Because my audiences receive insights and inspiration that improve their lives, both personally and professionally.

Thousands of people from both the private and public sectors have benefitted from my in-person or online training sessions.

In addition to helping improve your communication skills, I offer keynotes and workshops that focus on...

- Settling Your Self-Worth
- Creating an Inspiring Workplace
- Dealing with Difficult People
- Facing Your Fears
- Harnessing the Power of Your Thoughts
- Revealing the Pillars of Resilience

...and so much more.

Let's collaborate to make your vision a reality and your next meeting memorable.

Book Brenda Viola Today!

www.BrendaViola.com

Want More from Brenda Viola?

Could you use some support beyond the advice provided in this book? Visit www.BrendaViola.com for details about the following resources.

Coaching

One of my favorite things in the world is empowering clients through one-on-one communications coaching. Together, we can get the brilliance inside of you out of your mouth, while making sure you are well lit, sound great, and have stories and facts organized effectively. Just one hour can improve your communication skills forever, and, as a result, your confidence will soar.

Best of all, you'll be heard...without screaming!

Publications

My first book, *The Public Servants' Survival Guide*, is the basis for one of my most popular workshops. If you or your team are feeling stressed and nearing burnout, this book will show you the 10 contributing factors of burnout and how to correct your course to reclaim joy in work and life.

In addition, my children's book about friendship, *Annabelle the Octopus* (illustrated by my amazing sister, Shirlee DiBacco) is a sweet story that encourages little ones to reach out for help when they feel stuck and reveals that best friends can come in unlikely packages. "But nothing's impossible when love is there."

Newsletters and Social Media

When visiting my website, sign up for my monthly newsletter, which is a great source of encouragement. There's also a steady stream of ongoing content on all of my social channels. Access these resources by following this QR code:

Podcast

One more resource to mention is my podcast, *The Alchemy of Pain*. After facing a series of devastating losses between 2021 and 2023, and focusing on my own grieving and healing process, I became fascinated by the many people who have been dealt difficult circumstances in life.

In truth, haven't we all?

I wanted to learn from their stories. How did they cope? What did they learn? How did they change because of the difficult things they never would have asked for?

How did they "vici"?

I named my company Vici Communications LLC instead of Viola Communications because vici means "to conquer." And I believe my life's mission is to help people conquer, too.

The stories featured on my podcast are inspiring! My guests have faced a myriad of trials, and many have found their purpose through the pain. I know you will find value in listening and watching these episodes.

I close each podcast with an exhortation that will also end this book.

If you find yourself in a dark time, think of the caterpillar in the chrysalis.

It is a dark place, and I bet they wonder if they'll ever emerge.

When they do, it's not some graceful exit. A violent struggle ensues as they make their escape!

However, if the way was made easy and the chrysalis magically opened for them, the butterfly would still emerge, and it would still be beautiful.

But it wouldn't be able to fly.

It's the struggle that creates the strength in your wings to fly.

So keep pressing on in your dark season.

You are creating strength in your wings to fly.

And when you do, I'll be cheering you on.

"It's the struggle that creates the strength."

About the Author

Brenda Viola's favorite childhood Christmas gift was a tape recorder. She used it endlessly to interview anyone who let her, and her dream of becoming the next Diane Sawyer flourished.

Her innate curiosity, coupled with a knack for words, fueled the desire to make communication her profession. Forever grateful to her single mother, Bette Costello, who worked tirelessly to make a way for her daughters to pursue their dreams, Brenda graduated from Glassboro State College (now Rowan University) in 1985, with a BA in Communications specializing in Radio/TV/Film.

Working her way up as an intern at a local cable TV station, she soon became a reporter, talk show host, and anchor. An award-winning communicator and author, Brenda finds it humorous that clients are most curious about her brief career as a *QVC* show host!

In 2018, she created ME (Municipal Education) Seminars to address challenges faced by public servants. Her decade as public information officer for a Philadelphia suburb informed her well -received keynotes and workshops. This niche market grew organically with the 2020 publication of her first book, *The Public Servants' Survival Guide*. Audiences from both the public and private sectors resonated with the message that answered the question "How can you reclaim joy in work and life?" The 10 points outlined in the book continue to provide the framework for a transformative workshop helping participants recognize signs of burnout and change course. A Certified Virtual Speaker, Brenda Viola engages audiences effectively via camera or in person.

Corporate culture is a passion, and Brenda has built regional and nationally recognized workplaces. Helping companies define their core values, guiding leaders to infuse their teams with appreciation, and creating environments where people love to work are her specialties, now under the umbrella of Vici Communications LLC, formed in 2022.

Encouragement is at the heart of Brenda's messages, which are backed by extensive research and filled with humor and candor. Her personal stories of love, loss, and lessons learned open the door for her audiences to bravely reflect on their own lives. She sees breakdowns as gateways to breakthroughs, and she finds fulfillment serving as a catalyst for decisions that yield lasting, positive impacts.

A Philadelphia-area native, she resides in La Jolla, California, enjoying breathtaking views of the Pacific Ocean, relishing downtime to enjoy live music at the Belly Up in Solana Beach or sing karaoke (badly) at the Lamplighter. Her foodie exploits are documented on Instagram @eat_drink_lajolla, and her home away from home is Life Time, where dancing is her favorite form of exercise. A member of the National Speakers Association (NSA), Brenda's aim in life is to embody love—and to pet every dog that crosses her path.

Acknowledgments

Planned for publication in 2021, *How to Be Heard Without Screaming!* paused production in 2021. My mother's death in March of that year after a lengthy illness, followed by my beloved partner Mark's sudden passing, pulled the rug out from under me.

Despite the tragic interruptions, this book was meant to be written.

My personal healing coincided with other major life changes. Selling my home (with everything in it) in Florida; a move cross -country to San Diego, California; leaving my full-time work with a medical device company; and starting my life's dream, Vici Communications LLC, at the age of 59 proved it's never too late to start over!

Thank you to Weston Lyon, my publisher, for his patience during the "pause." And many thanks to my fierce and favorite female entrepreneur friend, Angela Pointon from 11outof11 in Ardmore, Pennsylvania. She introduced me to Weston, helping me fulfill my dream of becoming an author. A true friend in work and life, she is a model of grace, professionalism, and strength.

To the teachers who encouraged me to write, especially Mrs. Dodge in sixth grade, thank you for seeing potential in me. Teachers' work is often thankless except for the lives they change forever by their positive influences. (Side note: My dream is that every high school student gets a copy of this book, because learning how to communicate well will serve them all the days of their lives. How I wish I had found my voice in high school!)

I'd stack the communications education I received at Glassboro State College (Rowan University) on par with the best in the nation. I can still hear Ed Kasuba's voice in my head telling me to "edit, edit, edit" from his "Broadcast Journalism" class. Class-mates like Nancy Lowden Norman and Jim Koscs inspired me to be a better writer because *they* were so terrific.

One of the best things that ever happened to me was, at the time, one of the worst. How grateful I now am that my *QVC* career was cut short, or else I might be selling gold chains with lobster-claw clasps instead of speaking and writing to uplift people.

My work with Harron Communications, Lower Merion Town-ship, and Medical Solutions Supplier/Lympha Press honed my skills over the past 30+ years. Aside from the experiences gained, I made friends for life. Andy Walton from Harron Com-munications annoyed me with his brilliant writing ability. My Lower Merion Township Manager, Doug Cleland, irritated me by finding even the smallest error. They both made me far bet-ter at my craft, and for that, I am grateful.

The Chamber of Commerce's Leadership Main Line Class of 2004 gave me the wisdom and insights of Dr. Judy D'Angelo, to whom this book is dedicated. Another blessing from this experience? On day one, a team-building obstacle course showcased my comically poor athletic skills. In one exercise, we were partnered with a classmate who would spot us as we walked a tightrope. That partner's job was to keep us from touching the ground. I fell multiple times, but each time, I was "saved" by my kind partner, who became a friend for life. David Brennan continues to lift me up, now 20 years later.

San Diego has brought fabulous new people into my orbit. And one is an editor! Nadia Geagea Pupa, you are brilliant, and I'm so proud to call you friend. Fellow author Debbie Seid evoked a host of brilliant ideas over wonderful meals. Linda Anne Kahn and her husband David, son Paul, and daughter-in-love Nicole swooped in and became family to me. And my family here—Debbie and Craig Stevenson, their children John and Carolyn McClaskey and Andres and Colleen Perez, along with grandchildren Charlotte and Evelyn McClaskey make my heart swell with love and appreciation. Mary Jo/Grammy shows me how amazing you can be at 90!

Thank you to the Philadelphia Eagles for helping me find "my people" in San Diego, like Taryn and Ed Gillison and their family.

Then there is my unlikely bestie, Matt Josephson. The first person I met in San Diego, he has been my partner in all kinds of fun, like singing karaoke, building furniture for my apartment, dancing at the Belly Up, and dining ALL over. So smart, kind, and funny, and the embodiment of "free," he is a treasure to me. His future is so bright that I know I'll say, "I knew him when..."

The gap from Sarasota, Florida, to this new life I now live was huge and fraught with challenges.

Mark's sudden transition was difficult to bear, but the burden was lightened by the kindness of my Medical Solutions Supplier/Lympha Press family. Eric Ansart, Jillian Hampson, and Alexa Ercolano dropped everything to cover an important photo shoot for me, giving me space to just sit and cry. Joseph Carberry's extraordinary heart always let me know my well-being was the priority. And Steve Kantor? He's literally a magician, showing up on a white horse to make life better in any way he possibly can. How fortunate I am to call this man "brother."

Steve's better half is my sister from another mother, Renee Kantor. She, Cynthia Harcourt, Anita Hampson, and I are called "The Fab Four." These three amazing women each deserve pages of praise for the kindnesses shown to me during my dark days after Mark's transition. They drove (and flew) in immediately to be with me. As anyone who has suffered a great loss knows, there's no quick fix for grief. Whenever I needed a listening ear or a shoulder to cry on, they were (and are) my pillars. We go back, but we go forward!

The miraculous love and provision of Cindy and Peter O'Krepki, who literally moved in with me, readied my home for sale, provided emotional and physical support (and delicious meals), and helped me navigate the murky waters of grief and reinvention deserve everlasting thanks. They and Clickwell Media LLC are also the geniuses behind www.brendaviola.com.

Aside from my wonderful client, Lympha Press, Vici Communications LLC received a hearty boost from the friendship and support of Roseann McGrath. Many people wish you well in business. Roseann pulled out all the stops to set me up with key decision-makers and generously gave of her time to endorse my new venture. This is especially gratifying because Roseann doesn't offer a reference lightly. Her respect, both personally and professionally, means a great deal to me. (Plus, her husband Mike and parents Joan and Nick are also like family to me.)

Then there's the "family family" I'm so blessed to belong to. My niece, Deena Cook, and her son, Atlas, live in Nicaragua. We don't often see each other, but Deena's influence has impacted my life in lasting ways. A fiercely authentic woman, her devotion to honesty and truth led to my own awakening in 2017. My godson, David DiBacco, and his wife, Stephanie, are wonderful humans who I adore sharing epic dinners with. We pick "our song of the summer," and talk...and talk...and talk. We're more than family. We genuinely all like each other!

My brother-in-law, Tony, is a pillar in my life; a source of wisdom and joy who stars in many of my favorite memories. (And you should be so lucky to hear him do Elvis on karaoke nights!)

Which leads me to Shirlee DiBacco. I thank God every day that I get to live this life as your sister. No doubt I wouldn't have made it this far or weathered the many storms (and boy, there have been many) without your ever-present love and support.

Finally, taking a page from Snoop Dogg's speech when he got his star on the Hollywood Walk of Fame, I'd like to thank me.

(Are you laughing?)

I'm sort of chuckling, too...but I have to say it!

Here I am.

There were many opportunities to throw in the towel, to become bitter instead of better. I have experienced an aching loneliness and came to terms with liking my own company.

Stepping away from security, I started over, and it was hard.

And thrilling. And fulfilling.

I'm 60.

And I'm just getting started.

References

Annual Main Line Run/Walk. 2024. The Main Line Chamber of Commerce. https://www.mainlinerun.org/.

Apex. 2018. "How to Use Meditation for Laser-Focus." *Medium*, March 27, 2018. https://medium.com/@endibq/how-to-use-meditation-for-laser-focus-bc38f3c628ff.

Bareilles, Sara. 2013. "Brave" from the album *The Blessed Unrest*. Epic Records.

Brooks, Albert, dir. 1991. *Defending Your Life*. Warner Bros.

Burnett, Mark, producer. 2013. *Shark Tank*. Season 4, episode 13, "Episode 413." Aired March 1, 2013 on ABC.

Daniels, Greg, and Michael Schur, creators. 2015. *Parks and Recreation*. Aired 2009–2015 on NBC.

Daniels, Greg, dir. 2009. *Parks and Recreation*. Season 1, episode 1, "Pilot." Written by Greg Daniels and Michael Schur. Aired April 9, 2009 on NBC.

Davey, Lindsay. 2022. "Patient Guide to Self-Diagnosing Lipedema and Lipo-Lymphedema." *Toronto Physiotherapy*, March 15, 2022. https://torontophysiotherapy.ca/patient-guide-to-self-diagnosing-lipedema-and-lipo-lymphedema/.

Dogg, Snoop. 2018. "Hollywood Walk of Fame Ceremony." *Variety*, November 19, 2018. YouTube video, 1:15:39. https://www.youtube.com/watch?v=ytnAquLGBC8.

Donovan, Jeremy, and Avery, Ryan. 2014. *Speaker, Leader, Champion: Succeed at Work through the Power of Public Speaking, Featuring the Prize-Winning Speeches of Toastmasters World Champions.* McGraw Hill.

Ebbinghaus, Hermann. 1913. *Memory: A Contribution to Experimental Psychology.* Teachers College Press.

EF Hutton. ca. 1970. "When EF Hutton talks, people listen." Commercial.

Feig, Paul, dir. 2008. *The Office.* Season 4, episode 13, "Dinner Party." Written by Lee Eisenberg and Gene Stupnitsky. Aired April 10, 2008, on NBC. 22:00.

Kaplan, Gabe, and Sacks, Alan, creators. 1979. *Welcome Back, Kotter.* Aired 1975–1979 on ABC.

King, Carole. 1976. "Only Love Is Real." Track 4 on Thoroughbred. Ode / A&M.

"KYW Newsradio 1060 Commercial." 1991. YouTube video. https://www.youtube.com/watch?v=FyDxaFpmsEI.

Lipedema Foundation. 2024. https://www.lipedema.org/.

Love Language Brand. *Relationships Don't Have to Be Complicated.* Love Languages. https://5lovelanguages.com/.

May, Rollo. 1969. *Love and Will.* W. W. Norton & Company.

Mehrabian, Albert. 1981. *Silent Messages: Implicit Communication of Emotions and Attitudes.* Wadsworth.

Michaels, Lorne, creator. *Saturday Night Live*. Aired 1975–2024 on NBC.

One Thousand and One Nights. 1775.

Ruiz, Don Miguel. 1997. *The Four Agreements*. Amber-Allen Publishing, Incorporated.

Ryan Avery. 2024. Ryan Avery. https://ryanavery.com/ryan-avery/.

Shulz, Charles. 1950–2000. *Peanuts*. Syndicated comic strip. https://www.peanuts.com.

"The Short Reign of Suzette Charles: Suzette Charles Was Miss America for Only a Few Months but She's Taking That Brief Reign and Turning It into a Successful Career." 1985. *South Florida Sun Sentinel,* February 15, 1985. https://www.sun-sentinel.com/1985/02/15/the-short-reigh-of-suzette-charles-suzette-charles-was-miss-america-for-only-a-few-months-but-shes-taking-that-brief-reign-and-turning-it-into-a-successful-career/.

Toastmasters International. https://www.toastmasters.org/.

Viola, Brenda. 2023. *Annabelle the Octopus: A Story About Friendship*. Awesound.

Viola, Brenda. 2023–2024. *The Alchemy of Pain*. Podcast. https://www.youtube.com/playlist?list=PLi0xf2jvjWD_WF3SkEu6h5r3qK8UxVwqJ.

Winton, Jennie. 2019. "When It Comes to Your Message, How Much Is Enough?" Mission Minded, June 7, 2019. https://mission-minded.com/when-it-comes-to-your-message-how-much-is-enough/.

Zwick, Edward, and Herskovitz, Marshall, creators. 1991. *Thirtysomething.* Aired 1987–1991 on ABC.